CW00960193

20TH CENTURY COMPOSERS

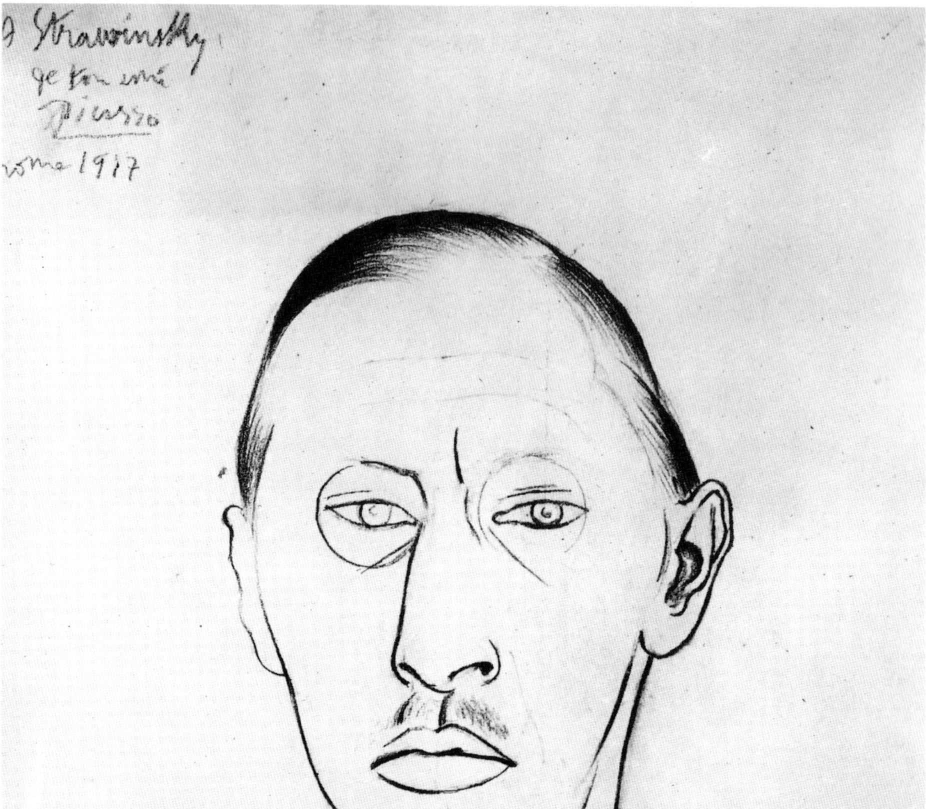
Stravinsky
Picasso
1917

Igor Stravinsky

by Michael Oliver

Φ

Phaidon Press Limited
Regent's Wharf
All Saints Street
London N1 9PA

First Published 1995
© 1995 Phaidon Press Limited

ISBN 0 7148 3158 1

A CIP catalogue record for this book is
available from the British Library

Printed in Singapore

Frontispiece, Stravinsky,
drawing inscribed 'by his
friend Picasso', Rome 1917

Contents

Preface

I first became aware of Stravinsky's music as a child of twelve or thirteen. I was astonished. It was quite unlike all the music that I then knew, and some of it was puzzling; but on discovering that some music-lovers disliked most of it, even denied its value, I already knew that they were wrong. Although the language was strange its physical impact and its power to communicate were breathtaking, and the realization that one of the great composers was my contemporary, and still composing, was deeply exciting. From then on I tried not only to hear as much of his music as possible but to seek out the first London performances of his new works.

The 1950s was a fascinating period in which to discover his music. Although the early ballets, even the once shocking *Rite of Spring*, were widely accepted as classics of the twentieth century, and the status of such later works as the Symphony of Psalms and *Oedipus Rex* seemed assured (though they were infrequently performed, and respected rather than loved) Stravinsky's neo-classical idiom had many critics. It was possible for such an arbiter of civilized taste as *The Record Guide* (by Edward Sackville-West and Desmond Shawe-Taylor; revised edition 1955) to describe such an enchantingly good-humoured work as the Octet as 'excessively theoretical ... recommended only to enthusiasts of Stravinsky's most poker-faced manner'. His dismissal by the conductor, composer and influential polemicist Constant Lambert (in *Music Ho!*, 1934) as a deracinated time-traveller 'whose executive abilities ... far [outweigh] his creative gifts' was widely shared. The idea that Stravinsky's music is dry, cerebral and cold is still not extinct, perplexingly to one who was drawn to it by its physicality, its joyous exuberance and its elegant wit.

On the other hand the partisans of Arnold Schoenberg and his school, then less numerous than Stravinsky's admirers, were already portraying him as a reactionary, wilfully blind to the inescapable forward direction pointed by the intellectual rigours of serialism. Before long, in some quarters, this had hardened to an orthodoxy that accepted only certain exploratory works of Stravinsky, excluding virtually all of the neo-classical ones. Stravinsky's gradual, wholly personal adoption and adaptation of serialism, which began in the 1950s, was received by this camp with satisfaction, by the older guard with contempt as the latest of Stravinsky's 'disguises'. To a schoolboy discovering the music at the time, discerning very little in the dazzling *Agon* or the poignant *In memoriam Dylan Thomas* that sounded like a homage to Schoenberg, very much that sounded recognizably Stravinskian, the heat of the controversy seemed artificial.

My realization of the true extent of Stravinsky's 'conversion' came with the rather more delayed dissemination of his strictly serial works. But by the time these had become relatively familiar, the modernist perception that the only possible destination for music's future lay on a line drawn through Schoenberg and his most radical pupil Webern (and thus including Stravinsky's early 'pre-Schoenberg' works, and his late, avowedly post-Webern ones) was being challenged. It was challenged not least by the works of, for example, Pierre Boulez, who could not deny his own debt to a tradition to which Schoenberg was foreign, that of Debussy. And thus the scene was set for our present perplexing but blessedly no longer doctrinaire Babel of styles and 'isms', with no perceptible central dogma or lingua franca.

Paradoxically it is Stravinsky and Boulez, despite their common inheritance from Debussy, who now seem the great irreconcilables of the twentieth century, not Stravinsky and Schoenberg. Boulez's doctrine of 'amnesia', of writing music that continually denies the past in its search for the future, is in direct conflict with Stravinsky, much of whose music is 'about' other music. Even his serial works represent an adoption of the past as part of his present; it is significant, however one explains it, that he showed no interest whatsoever in serialism until its inventor became part of the past by dying. Although the two were seen as opponents, Stravinsky's acceptance of serialism was no conversion to an opposing dogma. The greatest difference between them was that while Schoenberg was dogmatic, Stravinsky was not.

Accordingly we no longer need to sort Stravinsky's scores into 'acceptable' and 'unacceptable', and the biographer can feel free to include or omit in a study like this whatever works he pleases, without the need for defensive special pleading on the one hand or apology on the other. Stravinsky did write 'occasional' works, to oblige people or to make money, but listening to them all again, even those I had mentally docketed as 'minor', I have been surprised at how few of them I could decently ignore. In a century of violent change and of sometimes no less violent aesthetic controversy, Stravinsky was an astonishingly consistent composer, all the more astonishing for one who, despite all his attempts to demonstrate an intellectually coherent rationale behind his music, in fact wrote it for the most part with nothing but his ears and his imagination to guide him. At fifteen, I would have called him the century's greatest composer. For the next three decades or so, absorbedly investigating Schoenberg, Berg and Webern, to say nothing of Messiaen, Varèse, Shostakovich, Boulez, Stockhausen, Ives and a score of others, I would cautiously have added the phrase 'one of'. I no longer see the need for caution.

No composer of the century, not even Schoenberg, has been so voluminously written about. The bibliography at the end of this book is both an attempt to sift some of the most important sources from a confusingly large list, and an acknowledgement of those to which I have been most indebted. My other great debts are to Stravinsky himself, of course for writing the music but also for leaving a recorded legacy of performances that are in several cases still unsurpassed, and to Robert Craft (whatever the questions raised about the extent of his collaboration with Stravinsky on their jointly-written books) for providing the stimulus without which the masterpieces of Stravinsky's later years would perhaps not have been written.

There are established rules for the transliteration of Russian, but they are difficult to apply in Stravinsky's case. He spent the greater part of his creative career away from Russia, adopted French or English versions (often enough inaccurate) of the titles of his Russian works, and used Westernized spellings of the names of his relatives and friends. He referred, for example, to his first wife as 'Catherine' and to his eldest son as 'Theodore', and it would be confusing, however correct, to call them 'Yekaterina' and 'Fyodor'. Likewise I refer, as he did, to Serge Diaghilev, Léon Bakst and Alexandre Benois, not to Sergey Dyagilev, Lyov Bakst and Aleksandr Benua. Elsewhere I have only departed from 'traditional' spellings where they misrepresent pronunciation; thus I use 'Skryabin' (two syllables) instead of the more familiar but incorrect trisyllable 'Scriabin'.

Stravinsky for some years spelled his name with a 'w' in order to avoid mispronunciation ('Strafinsky') in German-speaking countries; I have ignored this, although his eldest son used that spelling. Titles of works are quoted in the form and the language in which they are most likely to be familiar to English-speaking readers, thus *The Rite of Spring* (not 'Le Sacre du printemps' or 'Vesna svyashchennaya'), *Les Noces* (not 'Svadebka' or 'The Wedding') and *Zvezdoliki*, not 'The King of the Stars' or 'Le Roi des étoiles'. This seems perhaps the best place to point out that if we are concerned about fidelity to Stravinsky's original titles, we should call *The Rite of Spring* 'Sacred Spring' or as he suggested 'The Coronation of Spring', that *Zvezdoliki* could better be rendered 'Star-Face' and that translating 'Svadebka' as *Les Noces* or 'The Wedding' ignores the fact that the Russian word includes an affectionate diminutive ending ('Little Wedding' will not do, 'Country Wedding' or 'Peasant Wedding' would be a little better). And it is high time that literal translations of Stravinsky's Russian-language works were made available. Not for singing: the sound of Russian words is an integral part of them, but the approximate translations of, for example, *Renard* and *Les Noces* that have occasionally and misguidedly been used for performances, and are all that are usually made available to the non-Russian speaker, quite disguise and bowdlerize the robustness of the originals.

Michael Oliver
London, 1995

I

'Dearer to my heart
than any city in the
world': Nevsky Prospect,
St Petersburg, 1901

*My childhood … was a period of waiting for
the moment when I could send everyone and
everything connected with it to hell.*

Stravinsky: *Memories and Commentaries*

Russian Spring 1882–1910

Igor Fyodorovich Stravinsky was born on 17 June 1882 (5 June
according to the unreformed Russian calendar; because the difference
between the Western and the Russian 'Old Style' calendar increased
by one day each century, for most of his life he celebrated his birthday
on 18 June). His birthplace was not the family home in St Petersburg
but a villa at Lomonosov, then known as Oranienbaum, a seaside
village on the Gulf of Finland which his parents had chosen for an
early summer holiday and no doubt as a healthy place for his mother's
confinement. Stravinsky was of Polish ancestry on his father's side,
from the Baltic provinces on his mother's, prosperously upper
middle-class on both. Numerous uncles and aunts owned large
estates; his father's library was said to be one of the largest and most
valuable in Russia. Fyodor Stravinsky (1843–1902) was the celebrated
principal bass singer at the Mariinsky Theatre, at the heart of St
Petersburg culture.

Stravinsky described his childhood as lonely and unhappy, but in
his otherwise minutely detailed recollections of that period he gave
few examples of what made it so. His father Fyodor, he said, was
remote, showed no affection and had an uncontrollable temper, but
this last seems to have been less of a physical threat than an occasional
public embarrassment; if his father ever struck him Stravinsky did
not speak of it. Anna Stravinsky, his mother, 'delighted in tormenting
me', but again he gave no instance of this, though later in her life
she too embarrassed her son by frankly expressing her distaste for his
music. His brothers (he was the third of four boys) 'annoyed' him,
but he did not say what form the annoyance took.

It is hard to tell whether this reticence hides genuine misery, even
cruelty, or whether like many another gifted child Stravinsky felt
alienated from his family's conventional respectability. His parents,
for example, seem to have had no strong religious beliefs, but nevertheless obliged their sons to go to Mass regularly. Stravinsky's older
brothers may have 'annoyed' him simply by their lack of interest in

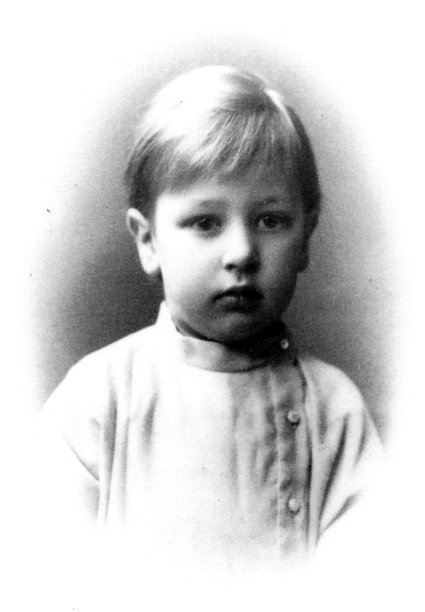

'Already a composer':
Stravinsky at four years
old, 1886

music. He was proud of the handsome Roman, eight years his senior, but he died while Stravinsky was still a boy. Of the next brother he had even less to say: Yury, three years older, pursued a successful career as a structural engineer, dying in Soviet Russia in 1941, but by then the brothers had not met or exchanged letters for over thirty years. On the other hand Stravinsky was very fond of his younger brother, Gury, no doubt partly because he too was musically gifted. He likened the room that they shared – and which Stravinsky seldom left in infancy because his parents believed his health to be fragile – to 'Petrushka's cell' where 'we found in each other the love and understanding denied us by our parents'. Gury's death, from typhus in 1917 while serving in a Red Cross unit during World War I, grieved Stravinsky deeply. He felt very lonely, he said, and was sad that Gury, who had a fine baritone voice and had begun to sing professionally, never had an opportunity to perform in public the two Verlaine songs he had written for him.

The only other relative that Stravinsky recalled with any affection was his uncle Alexander Yelachich, a high-ranking civil servant and wealthy land-owner who was also a passionate musical amateur, often spending days at a time at the piano. Two of his sons were musical,

The Stravinsky family at home, 1894 (left to right): Roman, Igor, Anna (mother), Yury, Fyodor (father), Gury

Stravinsky's parents: Fyodor
(standing) and Anna, 1896

too, and they and Stravinsky played duets together, including music
by Uncle Yelachich's musical god, Brahms. Stravinsky remembered
going on holiday to Frankfurt with his uncle, where he was introduced to the operettas of Johann Strauss.

The warmest relationships of his early childhood years were with
his father's butler Simon Ivanovich, who seems to have protected him
from some of Fyodor's severity, and with his German nurse Bertha.
German, he said, was the language of his nursery years (Bertha spoke
little Russian) and he used the language fluently, interpreting for his
parents on their summer holidays in Germany and, occasionally, for
German-speaking musicians visiting St Petersburg. He later engaged
Bertha as nursemaid to his own children, and when she died (in the
same year as Gury) he mourned her more genuinely than, many years
later, his own mother. As he began his eighty-ninth year, waking after
a night disturbed by dreams, he was upset that Bertha had not come
to wish him a happy birthday.

Although he began piano lessons at the age of nine, and made
rapid progress, Stravinsky said that neither of his parents recognized
musical talent in him. Perhaps this was all the harder to bear because
both were musicians. Anna Stravinsky was a more than competent
pianist, whose gift for sight-reading Stravinsky grudgingly admitted
he might have inherited. Fyodor, for his part, refused to allow his son
to study music, insisting that he pursue a legal career.

'The Slavonic language of the Russian liturgy has always been the language of prayer for me, in my childhood as now': St Petersburg, the Cathedral of Saints Peter and Paul, c. 1901

Stravinsky remained silent about whether this rejection was at the heart of his unhappiness as a child. His recollections concentrate instead, often with photographic precision, on the rich landscapes of sights and sounds that surrounded that childhood and remained with him throughout his life. His deepest and most indelible memories were of the city in which he grew up and the countryside in which he spent his summers. His love for St Petersburg was so intense that as an old man he said he was reluctant to look too deeply into his memories for fear of discovering how much of him was still joined to it: 'it is dearer to my heart than any other city in the world'. He described it as 'a realistic fairy-tale world whose lost beauty I have tried to rediscover later in life'. He did so most obviously in his ballet *Petrushka*, whose fantastic story takes place within a minutely detailed St Petersburg setting. But he also mentions his first opera *The Nightingale* and his later ballet *The Fairy's Kiss* as works in which

he tried to evoke his city. Neither is set in Russia, let alone in
St Petersburg, but both are magical fairy-tales (based on stories by
Hans Christian Andersen) with most equivocal happy endings;
both have a child-like profundity to them.

Nearest to the surface of his memory, he said, were the city's
sounds: hoofs and iron-rimmed wheels on cobble-stones, the cries of
street vendors, the bells of the Nikolsky cathedral, the mid-day gun
from the Peter and Paul Fortress, even the raucous shrilling of the
city's newly installed telephones (they sounded, he said later, exactly
like the beginning of Act III of his opera *The Nightingale*). All of
them are bright, sharp sounds; his great contemporary the poet Anna
Akhmatova gave a similar list to conjure up her St Petersburg. In her
Fragments from Memoirs she wrote:

> *Petersburg yard noises, First, the firewood being thrown through the
> cellar window. The organ-grinders … the knife-grinders … the old-
> clothes dealers … who were always Tatars. The tinsmiths … The noise of
> the bucket scraping on the well in the yards.*

If Stravinsky remembered his mother or his nurse singing him
to sleep, or the solemn chants of the Orthodox Church, he did not
mention them.

The visual allure of St Petersburg remained with him, too. In a
splendid, Pushkin-like phrase, he recalled his 'morning vision of …
the giant tsar and his giant coachman', breaking the spell by explain-
ing, now in the vein of Gogol, that Tsar Alexander III was 'a very
large man' (Stravinsky himself was a very small one), who on his
regular carriage drives past the Stravinsky family's apartment,
'occupied the entire seat of a droshky driven by a coachman as big
and obese as himself [whose] enormous behind, like a gigantic
pumpkin, was only a few inches from the tsar's face'. Another
transformation of memory into literature appears in Stravinsky's
evocation of the watery city's seagulls, where he turns from the precise recollection that they hovered lower when the waters were high
('when the city stood up to its nose in water') and the fish swam
closer to the surface, to the observation that 'a child does not wonder
why the sight of gulls should move him so deeply, but an old man
knows' (an old man, it should be said, who outlived most of his

friends and wrote their epitaphs in music) 'that they are reminders of death, and were such even when he watched them by the Neva one November afternoon when he was seven or eight'.

Death, in Stravinsky's later years, was a subject on no account to be mentioned in his presence. He was buried in Venice not because he had expressed the wish to be (though he loved the city), but because no one had dared broach the subject. A well-meaning admirer, presenting him with a photograph of Beethoven's death-mask, was dumbfounded by his paroxysm of rage and horror. Death was certainly a presence in his life from an early age. Convinced perhaps by his parents that his own health was precarious, he saw his father, two brothers, his first wife and one of his daughters all die before their time, several of them from tuberculosis. He too was subject to the disease, and although he lived until his late eighties he suffered illnesses frequent and serious enough for him to have contemplated death often. At eighty-six his last work was to arrange two songs by Hugo Wolf because he 'wanted to say something about death and felt that he could not compose anything of his own'.

He also remembered, and was not romanticizing when he acknowledged it as an influence, that St Petersburg is an Italianate city, in design, in material – marble and stucco – and in colour; he was often reminded of his 'ochre city' when in Rome. One facet of his music is indeed Italianate, or reflects Italy through the Italophile founding father of nineteenth-century Russian music, Mikhail Glinka. St Petersburg, though, was an Italian city surrounded by water and, often, by ice: skating and sledge-riding were among Stravinsky's earliest pleasures. But the thawing of the ice, so thick that it snapped and groaned as it melted in spring, 'the violent Russian spring that seemed to begin in an hour and was like the whole earth cracking. That was the most wonderful event of every year of my childhood.'

His favourite building in St Petersburg, whether glimpsing its domed roof from a corner near his home, walking into its blue and gold interior or simply watching its scenery being ferried by barge along the canal outside his bedroom window, was the Mariinsky Theatre (known later, in the Soviet period, as the Kirov). He was first taken there as a child of seven or eight, and was immediately enchanted. He remembered the 'perfumed' auditorium and the fact

Opposite, a modern view of St Petersburg by the River Neva: 'a city of islands and rivers'

'My most animated promen-
ades in St Petersburg were on
the Nevsky Prospect, a wide
avenue three miles long
and full of life and movement
all the way.'

St Petersburg: the Mariinsky
Theatre, where Stravinsky's
father was principal bass

that his family's box was decorated with winged cupids. In fairly
close succession he heard *A Life for the Tsar*, falling instantly in love
with the sound of Glinka's orchestra, and *The Sleeping Beauty*, the
beginning of a life-long love affair with ballet, and with the music of
Tchaikovsky. He had a persistent memory of the portico of the
Mariinsky swathed in black after Tchaikovsky's death, and of how
moved he was as the draperies billowed in the wind (did his
instinctive association of seagulls with death – the Russian word for
gull is *chayka* – date from that moment?). He was twelve years old,
and had seen the composer for the first and last time a fortnight
earlier, at a gala performance of Glinka's *Ruslan and Lyudmila*; it was
the opera's fiftieth anniversary and his father sang the role of Farlaf.
He saw Tchaikovsky only momentarily, and from behind, but
his white hair, broad shoulders and plump back remained another
abiding image.

Opposite, Tchaikovsky:
a photograph inscribed in
1888 to 'my dear and
deeply honoured friend
Antonín Dvořák'

    His first musical memories were much earlier. Throughout his
childhood, he would have heard his father practising and learning
new roles two rooms away from his own. But although Stravinsky
admitted that he had difficulty in putting his earliest musical
recollections in precise chronological order, the very first was probably military music from a marines' barracks near the family home.

He remembered, as soon as he was big enough to reach the piano keyboard, trying to imitate this 'bristling' music ('the tickling pleasure of my cradle-hood') and, when he failed to pick out the right notes, he recalled finding others that he liked better, 'which already made me a composer'.

Stravinsky's writings, especially the late series of transcribed conversations with his musical assistant Robert Craft, contain several unamplified but resonant statements of that kind. Did he really mean that he was in some sense a composer by the age of three or four (elsewhere he says that he began thinking of himself as a composer before his first music lessons)? It seems so, and in two senses. 'Preferring' or choosing one sound rather than another is in itself a definition of an important part of what composers do. And 'finding' or discovering musical ideas, finding them especially at the keyboard (Stravinsky almost always composed at the piano) was for him a crucial part of the composing process. Later in life he surprised a group of students by describing his pleasure at 'discovering' a particular chord. The chord in question was a perfectly commonplace one; he had discovered it afresh as the solution to a problem that it had not been asked to solve before.

Other ineradicable musical memories were of country people far from St Petersburg. He spent all his summers in the country, his ninth and tenth on the estate of his aunt Catherine, his mother's sister. At the great fair of Yarmolintsy nearby (Stravinsky compared it favourably to the ancient and much more famous fair at Nizhny-Novgorod), he saw and heard the peasant dances that he was later to use in *Petrushka*. Much earlier, but still retained in memory although only overheard while Bertha was taking him out for an airing, was the simple unison song of a group of village women on their way home from work in the fields. Not yet three and still slow at talking Stravinsky was able to repeat their melody so exactly that his father was surprised by the sharpness of his ear. He also delighted in remembering a simpleton, who could utter only two meaningless syllables, but sang them with fascinatingly virtuoso rapidity. Still more entrancing was the accompaniment to this 'tune', which the old peasant produced by placing the palm of his right hand under his left armpit, and pumping his left arm rapidly up and down. The boy attempted to imitate this effect ('which might euphemistically be described as resounding kisses'), with such success that he was sternly forbidden to make such indecent noises again. Without its accompaniment, however, he found that the two-note chant had lost all its charm.

By the time of his father's decree that he study law, music was at the centre of Stravinsky's imaginative life: he was spending four or five evenings a week at the theatre, he improvised at the piano for hours, and loved playing through his father's collection of scores, getting to know many operas in this way before hearing them in the theatre. Fyodor Stravinsky died, of cancer, relatively young, when his son was twenty. The two grew rather closer towards the end, and Stravinsky later excused his father's decision to send him to law school, admitting that before Fyodor's death he had composed nothing of consequence, and that his piano studies had progressed far enough to demonstrate that he would not make a career as a virtuoso.

He was no happier at school than at home, and made few friends there, though the impressive breadth of language teaching in Russian high schools – Stravinsky studied Latin, Greek, French, German and Church Slavonic as well as Russian (to the end of his life he prayed in Slavonic) – laid the ground for his later linguistic curiosity and his absorbed study of dictionaries in many languages. Nor did he enjoy his years at university, where his main studies were criminal law and legal philosophy, though again they may have left a legacy in the numerous lawsuits that he instigated later in life. By his own account he attended very few lectures, perhaps fifty in the four years of his course.

With one exception his closest friends were older than he was. Ivan Pokrovsky, already graduating from university while Stravinsky was still at school, 'dominated' his mid-teens, challenging his devotion to the Russian musical classics of which he had acquired a broad knowledge, and cultivating in him a taste for French music. They explored much of it together, including Delibes' *Coppélia* and *Lakmé* and Offenbach's *The Tales of Hoffmann*, in piano duet arrangements.

Stepan Mitusov became his 'literary and theatrical tutor' in Stravinsky's early twenties. They read Oscar Wilde, E. T. A. Hoffmann and Maurice Maeterlinck and saw the plays of Chekhov and Ostrovsky, Tolstoy and Gorky, as well as Shakespeare in Russian translation and many plays in French: there was a permanent French-

language theatre company in St Petersburg at the time, playing
Racine rarely but 'bad modern plays often'.

The one close friend of his own age was his first cousin, Catherine
Nossenko. According to Stravinsky the two realized that they would
marry from the moment they first met (when he was nine, she ten).
But he added, 'Perhaps we were always more like brother and sister.
I was a deeply lonely child, and I always wanted a sister of my own.
Catherine … came into my life as a kind of long-wanted sister in my
tenth year. We were from then until her death extremely close, and
closer than lovers sometimes are, for mere lovers may be strangers
though they live and love together all their lives … Catherine was my
dearest friend and playmate.' Indeed they look, in photographs
taken together, like brother and sister. There was a marked family
resemblance; Catherine in later years, her features sharpened by
illness, looked rather like a younger version of his mother, her aunt.

Stravinsky's musical studies were confined, not very systematically,
to his spare time. His father allowed him to receive harmony lessons,
but he found them irksome, wishing only that he had a better

Stravinsky with his wife
Catherine shortly after their
marriage in 1906

memory and could learn the tedious rules by rote and have done with them. (Although he eventually became an accomplished pianist, and even as a boy played Mendelssohn's G minor Concerto and much music by Clementi and Mozart, Haydn, Beethoven, Schubert and Schumann, he said that he lacked the 'performer's memory'; although in adult life he played in public only his own music, he had quite frequent memory lapses). Counterpoint on the other hand he liked, enjoying the practicality and discipline of solving its problems.

He began composing little piano pieces, and realized that he needed serious tuition. One of his fellow law students was the youngest son, Vladimir, of Nikolay Rimsky-Korsakov, Russia's most respected composer after Tchaikovsky and by far its most distinguished teacher. By now the Stravinsky family was in the habit of spending part of each summer in Switzerland or Germany, and on one such holiday Stravinsky discovered that Rimsky-Korsakov was not far away, visiting another of his sons who was a student at Heidelberg. Stravinsky was invited to stay (having already met Rimsky socially, as a friend of his father's) and showed the great man some of his pieces. He was neither enthusiastic nor dismissive but recommended that the twenty-year-old should continue with harmony and counterpoint, though not at the St Petersburg Conservatoire (where he would have lagged behind students of his own age, and besides: how could Rimsky, as a friend of Fyodor Stravinsky's, recommend that his son abandon his legal studies?); he added that his advice would be available if ever it were needed.

Fyodor died that autumn, and Stravinsky admitted that he felt a sense of freedom. He even attempted to leave home, until his mother staged a sufficiently convincing illness (and for a time sufficiently moderated her 'tormenting' of him) to draw him back, but he was soon spending as much time with the Rimsky-Korsakovs and their circle (including his new friend Mitusov) as with his own family. He later expressed repugnance at Rimsky's rejection of Orthodox religion, though at the time he shared it, as he did the older man's liberal political views. At a time of unrest in 1905, with widespread protests against the autocratic tsarist regime, Rimsky publicly took the part of his Conservatoire students, who had gone on strike, and was condemned by colleagues as a revolutionary himself. Performance of his works in St Petersburg was banned for a

Left, Rimsky-Korsakov:
a photograph taken by
Stravinsky in 1908 shortly
before his teacher's death

short period. (His last opera, *The Golden Cockerel*, was seen by the
censors as a satire on the incompetence of the regime, and was not
performed during his lifetime.)

It was at around this time that Stravinsky's other friend Pokrovsky,
together with a couple of like-minded acquaintances, founded a series
of 'Evenings of Contemporary Music', in an attempt to break away
from the stultified programming of the established concerts in
St Petersburg. They were not able to afford an orchestra, but at these
concerts Stravinsky encountered for the first time songs and chamber
music by Debussy and Ravel, Franck, Dukas and D'Indy, as well as
Brahms, Reger and Richard Strauss. He also heard a great deal of
Bach, and was even introduced to the then almost forgotten music of
Monteverdi and Couperin.

He began writing a piano sonata in the summer of 1903 and, running into difficulties, sought Rimsky-Korsakov's advice. The older
man may have sensed a talent emerging, for he now accepted
Stravinsky as a pupil, giving him two one-hour lessons every week
for the next three years. Stravinsky was already to some extent in
reaction against Rimsky-Korsakov and the 'picturesque' Russian
nationalism that he represented. Of the composers that Stravinsky
was now enthusiastically discovering, Rimsky distrusted Debussy,
saying that he preferred not to listen to him, since if he did there was
a risk that he might end up liking him, while he detested Strauss.
Tchaikovsky, the young Stravinsky's ideal, Rimsky could only see as a
Westernized rival. Stravinsky, however, seems to have realized how
much the old conservative could give him, and although he later
expressed many reservations about Rimsky's music, which he found
shallow, there were none about his teaching.

For the first eighteen months he was given exercises in orchestration, sometimes a passage from the opera Rimsky himself was composing at the time, *Pan Voyevoda*, much more often sonatas, string
quartets and marches by Schubert and Beethoven. Stravinsky had so
far written nothing for any instrument other than the piano; he
needed Rimsky's renowned and masterly knowledge of the orchestra.
No less important, his problems with the sonata demonstrated that
large-scale forms were as yet beyond him. Rimsky persuaded him to
start with something less ambitious, a sonatina, and then whenever
Stravinsky brought back an orchestrated classical sonata movement

Following page, 'I was
detained seven hours, but
seventy years will not
erase the memory of my
fears': a street demonstration
in St Petersburg in 1905, at
a time of widespread
unrest and general strike
following the disastrous
outcome of the Russo-
Japanese war.

for criticism, Rimsky would demonstrate how the piece was put together.

By 1905 Stravinsky had progressed far enough for his teacher to encourage him to start a full orchestral work. The Symphony in E flat, proudly labelled 'Op. 1' (and originally confidently entitled 'Symphony No. 1') was written under the master's close supervision, every few pages being taken to him for advice and comment. The work is a mixture of youthful influences, a tribute to Rimsky's teaching in its assurance, as well as in its sincere flattery and its affectionate dedication to him. Tchaikovsky is also present, as is Glazunov, the obvious model for any Russian symphony written at this period. There are also hints of Strauss, much more than hints of Wagner, as well as two indications, with hindsight, that Rimsky had also given Stravinsky the self-confidence to strike out in a personal direction. Two folk- (or folk-like) songs are incorporated, one in the second movement very close to an idea later developed in *Petrushka*, the other in the finale sounding rather as though Stravinsky had again remembered the old peasant with his simple tune and its exuberantly 'indecent' accompaniment (he later re-used this idea in a set of songs subtitled 'Memories of my childhood'; it is there called 'Tchitcher-Yatcher' or 'The Jackdaw').

The year 1905 was a significant one, with the Russo-Japanese war, an abortive revolution in Russia and mutiny on the battleship *Potemkin*. Stravinsky, although a passive bystander, was arrested one day during a student demonstration; he was held for several hours and never forgot his terror. It was also the year that he finished his legal studies and announced his engagement to Catherine Nossenko.

Marriage between first cousins was prohibited in tsarist Russia. It was necessary to find a priest who could be induced not to ask too many questions. One was eventually found, in a village outside St Petersburg, and the marriage took place early in 1906 without any guests save two of Rimsky's sons to act as best men and to hold the ceremonial crowns over the couple's heads. On their return home, they were greeted by Rimsky himself, bearing aloft an icon, which he later gave them. His other wedding present was the gift of his teaching.

After a fortnight's honeymoon in Finland, the newly-weds' first home was a pair of rooms in the Stravinsky family apartment. They

soon needed their own flat; their first child, Theodore, was born in
1907, their daughter Lyudmila a year later. Stravinsky also designed a
country house for his growing family near the Nossenko's estate at
Ustilug in Volhynia (a region of the Ukraine later ceded to Poland),
two-and-a-half days' journey by train from St Petersburg. The
property included a fair-sized estate, from which Stravinsky continued to receive income until the Revolution of 1917. It was at Ustilug
that he and his family spent at least part of each summer from 1907
until 1913, and where a great deal of his earlier music was written;
he became so attached to the place as a composing retreat that he
moved his grand piano there from St Petersburg. He already knew the
area: it had a salubrious reputation and he had been sent there for
several summer holidays as a child. It is somehow characteristic of
his parents that they did not trouble to accompany him.

On his honeymoon Stravinsky began setting a suite of three
songs for mezzo-soprano and orchestra, *Faun and Shepherdess*. They
disturbed Rimsky, with their apparent indebtedness to Debussy,
though the debt may be owed to Mussorgsky, some of whose
audacious harmonies were an acknowledged influence on Debussy.
Rimsky, whose editions of Mussorgsky's works had 'corrected' his
harmonic 'errors', would have cared for this influence no more than
for the other obvious ones of Wagner and Tchaikovsky. Stravinsky
thought that his teacher might also have been offended by the
absence of any of his fingerprints. Nevertheless he arranged for the
songs to be privately performed, together with the Symphony; the
almost immediate publication of *Faun and Shepherdess* may have been
his doing also. Stravinsky dedicated the beautifully limpid *Pastorale*
for wordless soprano voice and piano to Rimsky's daughter Nadia;
in retrospect it sounds like a first sketch for some of the poised, cool
melodies of Stravinsky's neo-classical phase of nearly twenty years
later and, like them, is indebted to his encounter with the music
of Glinka.

Rimsky spoke warmly to friends of Stravinsky's first independent
orchestral work, the *Scherzo fantastique*, but was critical to the
point of anger at the music and the sentimental texts, by Sergey
Gorodetsky, chosen for his next pair of songs, 'Spring' and 'A Song
of the Dew'. He approvingly looked over the sketches for what
Stravinsky planned to be his first stage work, *The Nightingale*, but of

the short and brilliant scherzo *Fireworks*, perhaps intended as a peace offering since Rimsky is again evident in its influences (and the work was intended, besides, as a wedding present for Rimsky's daughter and his favourite pupil, Maximilian Steinberg) he gave no opinion. The manuscript was returned, marked: 'Undelivered due to the death of the addressee.'

Stravinsky was distraught. He travelled for two days so that he might see Rimsky's face for the last time: 'He looked so very beautiful I could not help crying.' At least part of his later estrangement from the Rimsky-Korsakov family was due to a feeling that they had not grieved enough. Rimsky's widow, seeing him weeping, told him not to be so upset: 'We still have Glazunov.' Stravinsky said it was the cruellest remark he ever heard, and that he never again hated as he did at that moment.

He wrote a funeral dirge for Rimsky's memorial concert, the score of which is lost. A few months later the *Scherzo fantastique* and *Fireworks* were given their first performances. In the audience was Serge Diaghilev, founder of a hugely influential if short-lived avant-garde magazine, *Mir iskustva* ('The World of Art') and promoter in Paris of a much-discussed exhibition of Russian painting and a still more sensational season of Russian opera which included Fyodor Shalyapin's Western début in his most celebrated role, Mussorgsky's *Boris Godunov*.

Diaghilev was now planning to show Paris the riches of Russian ballet. He had already signed up the leading Russian choreographer Mikhail Fokine, and two distinguished visual artists, Alexandre Benois and Léon Bakst. He needed a composer, and on the strength of *Fireworks* his choice fell on the promising but still almost unknown 26-year-old late-developer Stravinsky. To be sure, the first work that the impresario gave him was something of a test of his competence: to orchestrate, for the ballet now known as *Les Sylphides*, two short piano pieces by Chopin and, for a now forgotten divertissement, another by Grieg. Stravinsky fulfilled the commission and had returned to the completion of *The Nightingale*, when Diaghilev approached him again, this time with a much bigger and more urgent task.

This was a ballet, intended for Diaghilev's second Paris season, on the Russian folk tale of the Firebird. The impresario's first choice of

The River Bug, near the Polish–Ukrainian border, on which Stravinsky went rowing every day in the summers from 1907 to 1912, from the riverside house that he had built nearby at Ustilug

composer had been Anatol Lyadov, who said he would take a year to complete it. The score was needed sooner than that, and besides, Lyadov had a reputation for not delivering on time.

Stravinsky was apprehensive – his only previous large-scale work, the Symphony, had been written piecemeal, at his own pace, and he was frightened by the deadline – but he accepted. The confirmation of the commission was delayed, he decided to take a brief holiday while waiting for it and before beginning this intensive spell of work, but in fact he began composing almost immediately, finished the 45-minute ballet in draft form in five months and finalized the orchestration a month later. As each section was written, it was given to Fokine to choreograph (they had agreed a detailed scenario in advance) and rehearsals were able to begin at once. The first performance, at the Paris Opéra on 25 June 1910, was an immediate and overwhelming success with both critics and public. Stravinsky became a major figure in the world of music overnight. 'The first *Firebird*! I stood in the dark of the Opéra through eight orchestral

The Firebird: Tamara
Karsavina as the Firebird
and Mikhail Fokine as the
Tsarevich in the costumes
by Golovine and Bakst
designed for the first
production, 1910

rehearsals conducted by [Gabriel] Pierné. The stage and the whole
theatre glittered at the première and that is all I remember.'

The Firebird, in the form of one or other of the suites that
Stravinsky extracted from it, was no less successful in the concert hall,
and for many years it was by far his most popular work. It was for
long a commonplace among those who disliked his later music to say
that Stravinsky never regained the genius of his early scores for
Diaghilev. Subsequently, as the stature of the later works became recognized, there was a tendency among some of Stravinsky's admirers
to depreciate *The Firebird* as immature and excessively indebted to
Rimsky-Korsakov. Stravinsky himself described its opulent orchestra
as 'wastefully large', and in later revisions reduced its lavishness, also
taking the opportunity to remove his more effusive expression marks
('passionately', 'with malign joy', 'mystically' and the like, all of
them quite uncharacteristic of the 'mature' Stravinsky, though embar-
rassingly characteristic of Skryabin, whose music Stravinsky's mother
made no secret of enjoying more than her son's).

The Firebird is the work of a young genius who has not yet formed
a mature style of his own but has already surpassed his teacher. The
orchestral virtuosity of the score is at least as great as Rimsky's own,
and though some of its effects are derived from him, others are
wholly original. From this point on Stravinsky's instrumental mastery
was absolutely secure, and he delightedly described his 'discovery'
of the magical sonority (near the beginning of the score) of strings
playing a glissando with the glassy sound of natural harmonics –
'which the bass chord touches off like a Catherine-wheel'. He was no
less delighted when such a master of the orchestra as Richard Strauss
professed astonishment at this sound, and 'instrumental mastery'
soon became one of the most unqualified terms of praise in
Stravinsky's vocabulary, a quality that he immediately recognized in
works as different (and as remote from his own artistic ideas) as
Schoenberg's *Pierrot Lunaire* and Debussy's *Jeux*.

In *The Firebird* Stravinsky also avoids his master's occasional
rhythmic squareness and is audibly on the way towards the nervous
and supple rhythm of his later works. Already, too, he is concerned
with thematic unity and, amidst all the dazzling colour and richness,
with an almost austerely thorough manipulation of small melodic
figures. This is the score's clearest pointer to what was to come,

The Firebird: Natalia
Goncharova's backcloth
for the final scene
in the 1926 revival

and it is already more than a step beyond and away from Rimsky-Korsakov's world. Composers seldom make their débuts with works of unprecedented originality; Stravinsky made his by writing what one might well call the last and greatest masterpiece of the Rimsky-Korsakov school.

2

Stravinsky at Leysin,
Switzerland, 1914

I was guided by no system whatever in Le Sacre
du Printemps ... *I had only my ear to help
me. I heard and I wrote what I heard.
I am the vessel through which* Le Sacre *passed.*

Stravinsky: *Expositions and Developments*

A Russian in Paris 1910–14

After the success of *The Firebird* and his second Paris season,
Diaghilev established his company on a permanent basis. He obviously needed a new ballet from the composer he had discovered and
suggested to Stravinsky that he consider a plot drawn from Edgar
Allan Poe. Stravinsky countered with an idea that had come to him
in a fleeting, day-dream vision while he was completing the final
pages of *The Firebird*: 'I saw in imagination a solemn pagan rite: wise
elders, seated in a circle, watching a young girl dance herself to death.
They were sacrificing her to propitiate the god of spring.' He had
talked about it to his friend Nicholas Roerich, archaeologist as well as
painter, known for his wide knowledge of Russian pre-history, and
he now suggested the subject as a ballet. At this stage it had no plot,
and was envisaged as a 'pagan rite symphony' with the working title
'Great Sacrifice'.

Stravinsky and his family spent the summer after *The Firebird* at
La Baule, a beach resort in Brittany (it was here that he wrote the
Verlaine songs that were intended for his brother Gury) and then,
since Catherine was pregnant again, they decided not to return home
to Russia, but to await her confinement in the healthier climate of
Switzerland. Their third child, a second son, Svyatoslav Soulima
(always known as Soulima, which Stravinsky believed to be the name
of one of his Polish ancestors) was born in a clinic at Lausanne.
Diaghilev, who visited Stravinsky there, was astonished to find him
working not on the planned 'Great Sacrifice' but on a sort of piano
concerto (Stravinsky called it a *Konzertstück*, no doubt remembering
Weber's work of that title). He had realized that the 'pagan rite symphony' was going to be a major undertaking, and wanted to 'refresh'
himself by writing an orchestral piece in which a solo piano would
have a leading role. While working on it, he thought of the piano as
a puppet suddenly brought to life, exasperating the orchestra with
diabolical flourishes, to which they reply with menacing trumpet-
blasts until, after a noisy climax, the unfortunate puppet is quelled.

Petrushka: costume design for the Ballerina by Alexandre Benois, 1911

After sketching one movement he racked his brain for a title, eventually finding exactly what he wanted in *Petrushka*, the Russian equivalent of Pierrot, Pulcinella or Punch.

After Stravinsky had played him a movement entitled 'Petrushka's Cry' and most of another called 'Russian Dance', Diaghilev was quick to realize the work's dramatic potential, and to suggest that the idea of the tragic puppet be expanded. They agreed on a plot-outline and a setting – St Petersburg's Shrovetide Fair – and Diaghilev, with equal shrewdness, suggested Alexandre Benois as collaborator, not only on the designs but also the details of the scenario. Benois was an

Above, Lydia Sokolova as
the Ballerina in a revival
of *Petrushka* in 1926
Opposite, programme for
Petrushka's première at the
Théâtre du Châtelet, Paris,
13 June 1911

Grande Saison de Paris. — Direction : G. ASTRUC & Cⁱᵉ

Les Ballets Russes

organisés par M. Serge de Diaghilew

DIRECTEUR CHORÉGRAPHIQUE
M. Michel Fokine

DIRECTEUR ARTISTIQUE
M. Alexandre Benois

PROGRAMME DE LA SOIRÉE

PÉTROUCHKA

Scènes burlesques en quatre tableaux de MM. IGOR STRAVINSKI et ALEXANDRE BENOIS

Musique de M. IGOR STRAVINSKI
Scènes et Danses composées et réglées par M. FOKINE. Maitre de Ballet
des Théâtres Impériaux de Saint-Pétersbourg.
Décors et Costumes dessinés par M. ALEXANDRE BENOIS
Décors exécutés par M. ANISFELD
Costumes exécutés par MM. CAFFI et VOROBIEV

La Ballerine.	Mme TAMAR KARSAVINA
Pétrouchka.	MM. NIJINSKI
Le Maure...	ORLOV
Le vieux Charlatan.	CECCHETI

Les nourrices : Mmes BARANOVITCH I, BARANOVITCH II, A. VASSILIEVA, M. VASSILIEVA,
GASHEVSKA, TCHERYCHEVA, LASTCHILINA, SAZONOVA, BIBER.

Les cochers : MM. LASTCHILINE, SEMENOV, PETROV, V. ROMANOV, ORLIK.

Les palefreniers : MM. ROSAÏ, A. MOLOTSOV.

Le marchand fêtard : M. KOUSSOV.

Les tziganes sans foi ni loi : Mmes SCHOLLAR, REISEN.

Les danseuses de rue : Mmes NIJINSKA, VASSILIEVSKA.

Premier joueur d'orgue : M. SERGHEIEV.

Second joueur d'orgue : M. KOBELEV.

Le compère de la foire : M. B. ROMANOV.

Le montreur de vues d'optique : M. OGNEV.

Masques et travestis : Mmes LARIONOVA, KANDINA. — MM. LEONTIEV, KREMNIEV,
OULANOV, S. MOLOTSOV, DMITRIEV, GOUDNINE, KOTCHETOVSKY,
MASSLOV, GUERASSIMOV, CHRISTAPSON, LAROSOV.

Marchands, marchandes, officiers, soldats, seigneurs, dames, enfants, bonnes, cosaques,
agents de la police, un montreur d'ours, etc.

authority on Russian puppet theatre, as well as a passionate enthu-
siast for the rapidly vanishing folk culture of the traditional fairs.

The Stravinskys had moved from Lausanne to a hotel at Clarens
after the birth of their son. For the winter months they moved again,
to Beaulieu, near Nice. Every afternoon under their window, a hurdy-
gurdy played a creaking little music-hall song, which Stravinsky
thought would be useful, and wrote it into his score at an appropriate
point – the appearance of a hurdy-gurdy man – in Scene I. He does

Petrushka: Tamara
Karsavina (Ballerina),
Vaslav Nijinsky (Petrushka),
Alexandre Orlov (the
Moor), Enrico Cecchetti
(the Showman), 1911

not tell us whether he knew at the time that the song's title was apt to a story about puppets: 'She Had a Wooden Leg'. It turned out that the tune was not traditional, as Stravinsky supposed, but the work of a certain Emile Spencer, whose publishers received a proportion of the royalties on *Petrushka* for many years thereafter.

Although the process of composition proceeded smoothly, it was not possible for Benois and Fokine, who were in St Petersburg, to hear the music until Stravinsky made a brief visit there for Christmas 1910, at Diaghilev's invitation but also to pay a duty call on his mother. He could not know it, but this was to be his last visit to his native city for over half a century. To his dismay, he found it 'sadly small and provincial' after Paris.

He returned to Beaulieu in the new year, but work was now interrupted for a month by an attack of what was diagnosed as intercostal neuralgia. Stravinsky dreamed that he had become a hunchback, and woke to find the dream almost true. The cause was nicotine poisoning; he was then, and would remain for many years, a heavy smoker. He completed *Petrushka* only in May, with the first performance due a month later. The finishing touches were made in Rome, where Diaghilev's company was appearing, and rehearsals began immediately, in the theatre's restaurant.

During rehearsals Stravinsky was delighted to go on excursions from Rome with Benois, 'a veritable education' for him, since the designer's knowledge of Italian art was profound. Benois himself has described how deeply interested in painting, architecture and sculpture Stravinsky was, unlike many composers of his acquaintance. He also recalled that although Stravinsky had no training in design or choreography he reacted wholeheartedly to his older colleagues' work in a way that they found valuable. In fact he was not ignorant of choreography, and in a musical milieu that saw Tchaikovsky's ballets as a waste of his time on a vulgar and evanescent art form, Stravinsky respected dance and did not see it as inherently inferior to opera. His hunger for learning, though, his omnivorous curiosity, were lifelong traits, from his early friendships with Pokrovsky and Mitusov to the delight he took in old age at Aldous Huxley's apparent omniscience and at W. H. Auden's ability to illustrate the most recondite verse-forms by improvising stanzas in them. And his need to know about the visual arts was professional:

Stravinsky always had an extremely clear idea of how he wanted his stage works to look. He counted *Petrushka* as a great advance on *The Firebird* for this reason, since in the earlier ballet he had been dependent on an imposed plot and a synopsis in which the choreographer, Fokine, had the major hand, whereas in *Petrushka* the dramatic conception and the musical form were his own, and closely related.

Petrushka is often bracketed with *The Firebird* as a work of Stravinsky's Rimsky-Korsakovian 'nationalist' phase. Although it is in many ways more intensely Russian than *The Firebird*, it actually represents his final break with his teacher's world. Orchestral virtuosity now gives way to a highly original re-thinking of the orchestra. Its colouring is more often pungent, even garish, than sumptuous; the comfortable warmth and stability of bass instruments are absent for pages at a time. The Rumanian–Italian musicologist Roman Vlad puts it well when he says that if Debussy's orchestra tends to sound like a harp, Stravinsky's in *Petrushka* seems to evoke 'a gigantic accordion or a broken-down fair organ'. He adds, though, that at the very centre of the score's fascination is its rootedness in the sonority of the piano. Stravinsky later arranged three dances from the ballet for piano, dedicating them to Artur Rubinstein, and it is astonishing how little the music is distorted or diminished in the transcription.

Petrushka uses folk melodies in a way that Rimsky would have approved but also, as in the case of 'She Had a Wooden Leg', urban demotic material that he would not. Indeed when Stravinsky asked Rimsky-Korsakov's son Andrey to send him a copy of one such popular Russian melody, it arrived with a set of derisive verses deploring Stravinsky's decision to use such 'trash'. Andrey later reviewed the score for a Russian newspaper, describing it as 'Russian vodka with French perfumes'. In one important sense *Petrushka* is indebted to Rimsky-Korsakov, while also indicating how far beyond his teacher Stravinsky had progressed. Rimsky in his last opera, *The Golden Cockerel*, had used the simple but effective device of portraying human characters with themes written in the 'normal' major and minor scales, and supernatural figures with music of an oriental-sounding, chromatic cast. Stravinsky had done the same in *The Firebird*, but more simply and more rigorously, exploiting the ambiguities that result when the two 'worlds' are placed in close

Petrushka: Stravinsky with
Vaslav Nijinsky after the first
performance

Stravinsky and Maurice
Ravel in 1913, during
their collaboration
on completing Mussorgsky's
Khovanshchina

Paris, 1910: Stravinsky
visits Debussy at his home
in the avenue du Bois de
Boulogne (photograph
by Erik Satie)

conjunction. This gives, for example, the music of the Firebird herself (a magical creature, but also the story's benevolent good fairy) an elusive, shimmering quality. When the chromatic and diatonic worlds combine, the music is effectively in two keys at once. Stravinsky had hinted even earlier, both in the *Scherzo fantastique* and in *Fireworks*, at a growing realization that this idea could be taken further. In *Petrushka*, where the principal character is both grotesque puppet and suffering human, the germinal idea from which the whole work grew (it now dominates the second scene of the ballet, 'Petrushka's Cell') is an angular motive for two clarinets playing simultaneously in two harshly conflicting keys. Such an effect was not entirely unknown, but the intention before *Petrushka* would always have been some kind of eventual resolution or healing of the inherent conflict. Here it is essential both to the drama and to the music that the only possible 'reconciliation' is an acceptance of duality. The two keys cannot co-exist except in a sort of 'super-key'. Again, the discovery is not entirely new, but it indicates how rigorously Stravinsky was examining the basic elements of musical language even in such a relatively early, colourful and popular score as *Petrushka*.

Again the first performance, at the Théâtre du Châtelet in Paris on 13 June 1911, was a triumphant success, not least for the startling realism and virtuosity in the title role of Vaslav Nijinsky (Sarah Bernhardt is said to have exclaimed 'I am afraid! I am afraid because I have seen the greatest actor in the world'). Stravinsky himself was pleased by the success and by the performance, conducted by the young Pierre Monteux, since it gave him an 'absolute conviction of my ear just as I was about to begin *The Rite of Spring*'. Debussy, now a friend and admirer, must have added to this confidence by a generous and perceptive letter referring to *Petrushka*'s 'orchestral infallibility'. Stravinsky was proud of Debussy's tribute to one particular passage in the score, where the sinister Showman first appears and brings his puppets to life: 'There is in it a kind of sonorous magic, a mysterious transformation of mechanical souls which become human by a spell of which, until now, you seem to be the unique inventor.' This short passage (it immediately follows the Showman's flute solo) is indeed extremely strange, even sinister, conveying perhaps that the magician's trick is more mysteriously evil than it seems: that his creatures, Petrushka at least, are in fact not puppets brought to life but living beings enslaved by his magic. Stravinsky always insisted that at the very end of the ballet, after the Moor has killed Petrushka and the Showman has reassured the horrified crowd by picking up the body and demonstrating that it is filled with sawdust, it is not Petrushka's ghost that appears on the roof of the Showman's booth, terrifying him with its bitterly derisive gestures, but Petrushka himself. It can be no coincidence that a strange echo of the music that so impressed Debussy recurs at this point.

Debussy had recognized Stravinsky's talent from the first. The range of other friendships made at this time is an indication of how rapidly he was accepted as a major musical figure, and of his wide interests outside music. Among composers, Maurice Ravel and Erik Satie, Florent Schmitt and Manuel de Falla became close friends; so did the writers Jean Cocteau, Paul Claudel and André Gide, and many painters, among them Pablo Picasso, Fernand Léger and André Derain.

Stravinsky had begun sketching ideas for *The Rite of Spring* in 1910, but he could not begin detailed work until a scenario and a visual conception were agreed with Roerich. Accordingly he returned to Ustilug in the summer of 1911, not long after Diaghilev's company ended their Paris season. He did not follow them on their first visit to London, where Diaghilev, uncertain of the notoriously conservative taste of the British, did not include either *The Firebird* or *Petrushka* in the company's repertory. From Ustilug he travelled to the estate near Smolensk where Roerich was staying, and on his return he began *The Rite of Spring* in earnest, starting with the first scene of Part I, 'Auguries of Spring'.

Curiously enough, considering his realization that *The Rite* would be a major undertaking, and his expectation that Diaghilev would need the score by the spring of 1912 (in the event the première was postponed), Stravinsky worked simultaneously during the summer of 1911 on two other compositions. The two brief songs to poems by Konstantin Balmont might be considered a relaxation from *The Rite of Spring*, but the extraordinary cantata *Zvezdoliki* (usually translated as 'The King of the Stars', the title actually means 'Starry' or 'Star-faced') could be no such thing; indeed as late as 1959 Stravinsky described it as 'in one sense my most "radical" and difficult composi-

Vaslav Nijinsky as the faun
in L'Après-midi d'un faune,
1912

tion'. A brief and mystically visionary cantata for male voice chorus and an enormous orchestra, it was dedicated to Debussy, who was flattered but puzzled, predicting that it might receive performances on a distant star, but not on 'our more modest Earth'. He was right: the choral parts, ambiguous of key and hideously difficult for singers to pitch accurately, were long thought to be unsingable; the work remained unheard for over a quarter of a century. And yet, now that choral singers have discovered that it is possible, *Zvezdoliki* is another demonstration of the precision of Stravinsky's ear: perhaps without concerning himself too much about problems of performance, he heard and found a means of writing down these mysterious, veiled sonorities.

Zvezdoliki has often been described as a sort of sketch for *The Rite of Spring*, and so far as harmonic vocabulary is concerned this is true. But it is a remarkable demonstration of how fundamental Stravinsky's investigations of musical language were, and how fast they were proceeding, that the two works should sound so utterly different: *The Rite* all savage force and violently syncopated rhythmic energy, *Zvezdoliki* remote and mostly quiet, ritually static. Even the harmonic trait that they share (a liking for the simultaneous sounding of adjacent chords) has a quite different effect: tense dissonance in *The Rite*, an almost motionless shimmer in *Zvezdoliki*. Only in their virtuoso imagining of strange and novel sonorities are the two works obviously by the same composer.

Stravinsky, back in Clarens, had almost completed Part I of *The Rite of Spring* by Christmas 1911, when Diaghilev decided to postpone its première for a year. Part of the reason, no doubt, was that he did not want to overwhelm his forthcoming Paris season with novelties, and four new ballets were already planned. But he was also grooming Nijinsky, his leading male dancer (and his lover), as a choreographer. He wanted Nijinsky to choreograph *The Rite*, but he was taking so long over a version of Debussy's *Prélude à l'après-midi d'un faune* that there would clearly not be time for both.

Stravinsky was disappointed, but on the whole glad of the opportunity to continue work on *The Rite* with less pressure. It gave him the leisure to attend Diaghilev's Paris season in May 1912, where he was impressed by Fokine's *Daphnis et Chloé* to a commissioned score by Ravel. He gave conflicting accounts of his reaction to

Nijinsky's *L'Après-midi*, dismissing it rather coldly in the *Chronicles of my Life* that he published in the mid-1930s, but twenty-five years later confessing that he 'adored' it. At the time of the earlier judgement Stravinsky may still have been in some sense blaming Nijinsky for the notoriously violent reception of *The Rite*, and at that time also he was at the height of his neo-classical phase, which included a deep commitment to the purest classical choreography. He may also have felt that *L'Après-midi* was a warning that he ought to have heeded: the most talked-about feature of its choreography was a simulated orgasm that deeply shocked some of the first-night audience.

Stravinsky attended Diaghilev's second London season, where *The Firebird* was successfully produced, followed the dancers to Venice and Budapest, and in the autumn visited Berlin for the local première of *Petrushka*. Here the paths of the two greatest creative forces in twentieth-century music crossed for the first time. Arnold Schoenberg was in the audience for one of the performances of *Petrushka*, a few days later Stravinsky heard Schoenberg's *Pierrot Lunaire*, and they seem also to have met socially. Stravinsky was clearly impressed by *Pierrot*: in an interview a few weeks later he described Schoenberg as 'one of the greatest creative spirits of our era'. They did not speak to each other again. Professional rivalry was no doubt part of the reason, sharpened by the 'Schoenberg *or* Stravinsky?' factionalism that grew up among their admirers. Schoenberg later came to resent Stravinsky's comparative commercial success. Stravinsky usually avoided discussing Schoenberg, saying only that 'he is too far from my aesthetic'. In an interview in the USA, though, he spoke rather loftily of composers who were trying to write 'the music of the future', saying that he preferred to compose for the audience of today. Schoenberg was furious, wrote a satirical poem about 'little Modernsky with his real false hair just like Papa Bach' – Stravinsky was deep into his neo-classical phase by this time – and set it to music. Stravinsky always retained his admiration for *Pierrot*'s instrumental mastery, and after Schoenberg's death, his references to Schoenberg's other works grew ever warmer. He was at last to adopt, albeit in a highly individual manner, Schoenberg's twelve-note serial technique.

Between trips to London and Berlin, Stravinsky returned to Ustilug to continue work on *The Rite*, breaking off for a brief visit, at

Diaghilev's invitation, to hear Wagner's *Parsifal* at Bayreuth. He was
repelled, especially by the quasi-religious atmosphere prevailing at the
festival, a feeling that *Parsifal* was more than a work of art, in some
way a religious observance. Stravinsky was at this time an agnostic,
having rejected the Orthodox faith as a schoolboy, but in his
revulsion at *Parsifal* we can perhaps detect not only his distaste for
Wagner's grandiloquence but the first twinges of his later return
to Christianity.

By the end of 1912 *The Rite* was all but finished. The dancers began
rehearsing Nijinsky's choreography while they were still on tour
and Stravinsky was putting the finishing touches to the scoring. The
number of rehearsals Nijinsky called is legendary – some accounts
suggest as many as two hundred – and together with Stravinsky's
remarks about Nijinsky's musical illiteracy and the fact that the most
notorious ballet in history had only six performances (Diaghilev's
revival of it was to new choreography by Leonide Massine) has led to
an impression that Nijinsky's work was incompetent. In recent years
however his choreography has been reconstructed, based on lightning
sketches drawn at the original performances by the young artist
Valentine Gross, on the memories of Nijinsky's sister Bronislava
Nijinska – herself a choreographer of great distinction, with whom he
tried out many of the steps – and on the detailed notations of Marie
Rambert, then an expert in Dalcroze eurhythmics who had been
engaged by Diaghilev as Nijinsky's assistant. Two things seem clear
from this reconstruction. First, Nijinsky was attempting a revolution
in choreography of a kind comparable to that of such later pioneers
of modern dance as Martha Graham. He was emphasizing weight
instead of lightness; at rest his dancers had their toes pointing
inwards, their knees touching and their elbows clamped to their
sides, all disconcerting denials of the classical 'first position'. He
also seems to have been making a genuine attempt to create physical
patterns in space that echoed the patterns, even the different
instrumental colours, of Stravinsky's music.

The Diaghilev company had been invited to open the brand-new
Théâtre des Champs-Elysées in the late spring of 1913. Diaghilev
seems to have sensed that *The Rite* might provoke protest, so he chose
not to open the season with it, selecting instead Debussy's *Jeux*, the
choreography of which had been devised by Nijinsky in the weeks

1913

Stravinsky playing *The Rite of Spring*: drawing by Jean Cocteau

after finishing work on Stravinsky's ballet. *Jeux* was coolly received, but a spectacular revival of Mussorgsky's *Boris Godunov* restored the company's hold on the public. A fortnight into the season, on 29 May, *The Rite* eventually appeared, cautiously surrounded by popular ballets featuring star soloists. (*The Rite* was one item in a quadruple bill of *Les Sylphides*, *Le Spectre de la rose* and the Polovtsian Dances from Borodin's *Prince Igor*, with Karsavina, Nijinsky and Adolph Bolm in principal roles.) Stravinsky always insisted that he was surprised by its riotous reception. 'The music was so familiar to me; I loved it, and I could not understand why people who had not yet heard it wanted to protest in advance'. There were sounds of mild protest even during the Prelude. When the curtain rose 'on the group of knock-kneed and long-braided Lolitas jumping up and down, the storm broke'.

The hubbub was increased by counter-protests. At this new theatre the standing room, occupied by the young, impecunious enthusiasts for all that was new, was placed between the most fashionable boxes and the stalls. Stravinsky left the auditorium in a rage, arriving backstage to find Nijinsky standing on a chair shouting numbers to his dancers, who could not hear the orchestra above the din, while Diaghilev gave instructions for the house-lights to be switched on and off in a vain attempt to restore order. In the auditorium there were satirical calls for a doctor ('No, two doctors! A dentist!') as the dancers went through their spastic movements. One member of the audience recalled that it took some time to realize that his head was being pounded by the fists of the person seated behind him. An elderly aristocrat, her tiara awry, stood up in her box crying that in sixty years she had never been so insulted, while Stravinsky's friend the composer Florent Schmitt roared at the society ladies in the audience 'Taisez-vous, garces du seizième!' (almost literally, 'Shut up, you Berkeley Square bitches!').

After the tumult was over Stravinsky and Diaghilev, with a group of friends, went for a nocturnal stroll in the Bois de Boulogne. Jean Cocteau, who was present, left a highly romanticized account of Diaghilev tearfully reciting Pushkin; Stravinsky's recollection was that all the impresario said was, 'Just what I wanted.'

Curiously enough there was no repetition of these disorderly scenes at the later performances, either in Paris or in London, while the first concert performance, a year later, was as triumphant as the first night had been disastrous: the applause was overwhelming and Stravinsky was carried through the streets of Paris on the shoulders of a young and wildly enthusiastic crowd of admirers.

Apart from Nijinsky's choreography, the reasons for the initial outrage were that the music was intensely dissonant, its powerful rhythms disconcertingly asymmetrical. The two phenomena are connected, and the link is one reason for *The Rite*'s position as the century's most liberating, trail-blazing and revolutionary work of music. In a conventional nineteenth-century harmonic context the risk of intense dissonance, however momentarily colourful or expressive it may be, is that it robs the music of a sense of movement. Where a chord is so dissonant that the ear cannot sense a possible resolution, the music stands still. Stravinsky's achievement, and it was unprecedented, was to give a crucial structural importance to rhythm instead of harmony, and to use the tension of dissonance to fuel this powerful engine still further.

The Rite of Spring:
Stravinsky's manuscript
of the full score

Left and below, sketches
made at performances of
The Rite of Spring, 1913,
by Valentine Gross, cued
to the appropriate bars of
the score

Right and *opposite*, two of
Nicholas Roerich's costume
designs for *The Rite* of
Spring. Many members of
the audience found the
smocks and leggings, hiding
the dancers' legs, as
disagreeable as Nijinsky's
revolutionary choreography

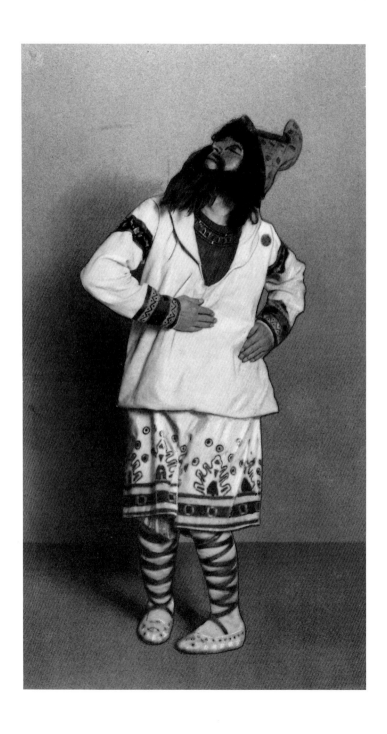

Another of *The Rite*'s innovations is its way of using melody. Its basic melodic ideas are usually simple and very brief, made up of very few notes. Some are derived from folk-song, but of a type in which short melodic cells are flexibly permutated. Stravinsky wrote melodies of this kind himself, often repeating a phrase with the addition of an extra note to alter its length and rhythm. Thus melody is also intimately linked with the work's rhythmic power.

The Rite of Spring established Stravinsky, already world famous since *The Firebird* and *Petrushka*, as a leader of the avant garde. It must have been very hard, even for the composer himself, to predict where he would turn next. The sheer richness of incident, extravagance of orchestral resource and barbaric power of *The Rite* were unrepeatable. After a severe attack of typhoid fever and a period of convalescence, followed by the domestic disruptions caused by his wife becoming ill and the birth of their fourth child (a daughter, Maria Milena, usually known as Milène) three options gradually offered themselves, of which the most attractive financially was the one that least appealed to Stravinsky. His opera *The Nightingale*, set aside in order to write *The Firebird* and untouched in the intervening five years, had aroused the interest of a newly formed theatre company in Moscow. The first act, sketched while Rimsky-Korsakov was still alive, was written in a style to which Stravinsky knew he could not return. He offered the first act on its own, but the offer was

The Rite of Spring, Paris
1913: *left and above*, two
contemporary sketches by
Emmanuel Barcet

refused. Jean Cocteau, meanwhile, was pursuing him with an idea
for a ballet set in a fairground, to be called 'David'. In his own mind
Stravinsky was already formulating *The Rite of Spring*'s true successor,
Les Noces ('The Wedding'). Diaghilev, as soon as the idea was
explained to him – a dance drama based on Russian peasant wedding
customs – was eager to commission it.

The Moscow Free Theatre, however, offered the composer a fee
of ten thousand roubles, a vast amount and far more than Diaghilev
could pay. Stravinsky, with some reluctance, began not only to compose the second and third acts but to revise the first so that the
inevitable clash of styles would be less glaring. Before the score was
finished the Moscow Free Theatre went bankrupt, though not before
paying Stravinsky's fee. Diaghilev offered to stage the work himself,
and Stravinsky was free to contemplate *Les Noces*. (As for the Cocteau
scenario, never much to Stravinsky's taste, it surfaced four years
later as *Parade*, with music by Erik Satie, sets by Picasso and choreography by Massine).

The Nightingale (staged in Paris in May 1914 and in London in
June) was no more than politely received, despite a fine performance
and exquisite designs by Alexandre Benois. Audiences may have been

The Nightingale: design
(1914) for the Emperor's
throne-room (scene 2) by
Alexandre Benois

expecting a shocking successor to *The Rite of Spring* and the opera was overshadowed by one of Diaghilev's undoubted triumphs, the first performances in the West of Rimsky-Korsakov's last opera *The Golden Cockerel* in a danced version, the singers placed at the side of the stage. The delicate orientalism of Stravinsky's work may have paled beside his master's, especially since both operas feature exotic marches and processions and a leading role for high coloratura soprano. In later years Stravinsky expressed dissatisfaction with his work, preferring the first act, 'which at least is operatic' to its successors, which he termed 'a kind of opera–pageant ballet'. When Diaghilev suggested reviving the opera as a ballet, Stravinsky countered with a proposal that he should condense the second and third acts only into a symphonic poem that could also be used for choreographic purposes. It was produced as *The Song of the Nightingale* in 1920.

Both versions, despite much that is picturesque and melodically charming, and a dream-like magical quality that must owe something to Stravinsky's childhood memories of theatre in St Petersburg, were essentially distractions from finding a way forward from *The Rite*. Audiences that found the succession *Petrushka | Rite | Nightingale* puzzling were to be quite baffled by the next work, where that way forward was definitively signalled – the Three Pieces for String Quartet which Stravinsky wrote in the late spring and summer of 1914.

They are rarely programmed in concerts of chamber music, no doubt because of their profoundly 'un-quartet-like' nature, and have therefore been little-known until recent years. They take the melodic language and techniques forged in *The Rite* to an extreme. In the first piece, later subtitled 'Dance', the first violin has a tune, simply repeated without variation, using only four notes. The cello, no less repetitiously, is given a brief rhythmic figure which again is never varied. The violin's theme is twenty-three beats long, the cello's rhythmic figure seven. Thus the piece is almost a mathematical formula for unpredictability. The pattern would only begin to repeat itself on the sixth repetition of the violin melody, and the piece ends before that point is reached. The viola has only a single note throughout; the second violin begins and ends by playing the same note, for the rest of the time increasing the unpredictability by sporadic repetitions of a descending figure of four notes. The piece denies the perceived nature

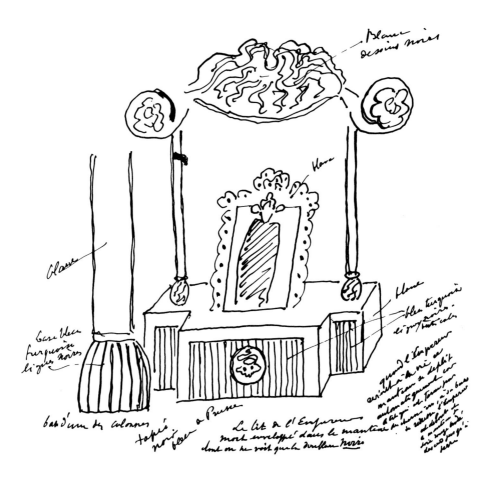

The Song of the Nightingale: designs (1920) by Henri Matisse for the Emperor's Dancers and the Lantern Carriers, *opposite;* and the Emperor's bed, *above.* The inscription explains that when the Emperor lies dead only the black lining of his cloak is visible, but as he comes back to life the hinged back of the bed rises until he is standing, the embroidered red silk of the cloak now falling to the ground.

of the string quartet in that there is no dialogue between the instruments whatever: each persists obsessively with its own material.

In the second movement, 'Eccentric' (inspired by the jerky movements of the clown Little Tich), lurching chords are abruptly juxtaposed with a tiny insouciant fragment of a tune, like something one might whistle absent-mindedly; a wider-ranging idea, though scarcely longer, provokes a paroxysm of atonal wrigglings. The remarkable third piece, 'Canticle', somewhere between a quiet chorale and a mysterious procession, is simultaneously a searching examination of dissonance and a remote and ghostly echo of Russian Orthodox chant. The Three Pieces, barely seven minutes long in total duration (of which the hypnotic third piece accounts for more than half), are a research laboratory in which Stravinsky tested the discoveries of *The Rite* and proved their validity in quiet music as well as loud, in monochrome as well as colour, in miniatures as well as great orchestral landscapes. They were to prove crucial for his continued development, and echoes of them are heard throughout the music of his remaining five creative decades.

3

Portrait of Stravinsky (1915)
by Jacques-Émile Blanche

*The greatest single crisis in my life as a composer
was the loss of Russia, and its language not only
of music but of words.*

Stravinsky: *Themes and Conclusions*

Exile 1914-20

The year 1914 struck Stravinsky a double blow. He had been
exempted from military service on health grounds, so did not have to
return to Russia to enlist, but the operation of Diaghilev's company,
his main source of income, became impossible. Royalties from
concert performances diminished severely and besides, his publisher's
agents in Western Europe were a German firm. Access to funds and
property in Russia became difficult; then, with the Easter Revolution
of 1917, impossible.

His worries were increased by the state of his wife's health. Just
before the war began Catherine Stravinsky was diagnosed as suffering
from tuberculosis. There may well have been signs of it earlier,
since Stravinsky referred late in his life to her 'fifty-year struggle' with
the disease (she was fifty-nine when she died). She was sent to a sanatorium in Switzerland, which therefore seemed an obvious wartime
base, as well as a safer one than France, and the family made their
home there for the next six years. Stravinsky must have realized that
his separation from Russia would be prolonged. His mother, though,
was anxious to return, and did so as soon as transport could be found.
At the same time Stravinsky arranged for his old nurse Bertha, his
'second mother', to join his family in Switzerland.

On his last visit to Russia, just before the war, he went to great
trouble to obtain a published collection of peasant wedding songs.
His library already contained volumes of folk poetry, some of it
drawn from an ancient, almost extinct tradition of popular drama.
There is also clear evidence, though he later denied it, that he was
studying Russian folk music. As early as the Spring of 1913, he said
later, his notebooks 'began to fill with notations for songs'. All of
them have a marked Russian flavour, but he seems to have been
trying to distil from folk-song some essence that would be in accord
with the flexible, narrow-range melodic language that he had begun
to forge in *The Rite of Spring*, rather than using 'real' traditional
melodies. One of the sketches of this type appears on the same leaf as

Stravinsky's jotting-down of the chimes of St Paul's Cathedral in London, heard from a cab that he was sharing with the British critic Edwin Evans. According to Evans, Stravinsky stopped the cab in order to listen absorbedly to these sounds 'in which he claimed to hear the most wonderful music'. Stravinsky found that the bell notations when written down looked 'remarkably Russian'. They do not, in fact, but his annotation on the sketch-leaf, as well as the way the three lines of bell motifs are laid out, make it clear that it was the 'astonishingly beautiful *counterpoint*' (his phrase, my italics) of presumably several sets of church bells ringing at once that stirred him. To him they sounded 'remarkably Russian' because the Russian technique of bell-chiming, in which the ringers struck the bells directly with hammers, or by using short cords attached to the clappers, encouraged simple counterpoint (albeit with complex dissonances due to the rich overtones characteristic of bells) even from the bells of a single tower. In Britain, where the technique of ringing bells by swinging them with long ropes operated from ground level made synchronization all but impossible, he could only have heard such sounds in a place like the City of London where two or more sets of bells were rung in close proximity.

Wartime economics seriously reduced the market for large-scale choral and orchestral music. After *The Rite of Spring*, disregarding the reluctant completion of *The Nightingale*, Stravinsky wrote nothing for symphony orchestra for many years. But writing for smaller groups was also musically necessary to him as a means of exploring the new territory opened up by *The Rite*. In the Three Pieces for String Quartet he took the first bold steps in that exploration. Thus a complex of reasons led to what is often called Stravinsky's 'Russian phase'. Another contributory factor, sharpened by his exile not only from Russia but from his native tongue, was an absorbed study of the musical characteristics of the Russian language.

He had noticed that in Russian folk music the natural accentuation of the spoken language is often ignored. He described this as 'one of the most rejoicing discoveries of my life', since not only did it have an obvious affinity with the ever-shifting accents of his recent music but it also enabled him to set Russian verse for the pleasure of its individual sounds and their cadences (which produce, he said, 'an effect on one's sensibilities very closely akin to that of music'), as well

Stravinsky, Diaghilev,
Cocteau and Satie,
caricature by Mikhail
Larionov, c. 1923

as to enjoy the language's rich propensity for ambiguity and punning,
verbal games and nonsense. The work towards which all this was
directed was *Les Noces*, but there seemed no possibility of Diaghilev
being able to stage it in the foreseeable future. The notebook full of
ideas for songs, and the detailed study of folk texts, bore fruit in a
sequence of short works that seem as remote as possible from the
Swiss countryside in which Stravinsky now found himself. They
include *Pribaoutki* (the 'official' translation is 'Pleasant Songs', but
Stravinsky explained that the Russian word really means 'tellings', a
popular verse form in which the text passes from singer to singer at
great speed, each uttering a single word), the *Cat's Cradle Songs*, the
Three Tales for Children and the Four Russian Peasant Songs (known
as 'Saucers', using texts from an ancient peasant ritual in which
personal objects, placed in a dish and covered by a towel, are
extracted to the singing of allegorical texts, their owners' fortunes
being divined from the words reached at that point).

   The last of this group of earthily pungent miniatures is the Four
Russian Songs of 1918/19, and of these the most remarkable is the
fourth, 'Sektanskaya'. The text was collected among a dissident
religious sect, and describes the sinner cut off from God: 'Snowstorms

and blizzards close all the roads to Thy Kingdom. Closed are all paths to my Father.' Stravinsky's wailing lament of a setting sounds like a passionate farewell to Russia, perhaps also a yearning for religious faith, and a discovery of the intensity that can be drawn from minimal resources, rigorously explored. The vocal range of the song is very narrow, but within this limit the voice obsessively ululates from note to note. Stravinsky had little to say about this song, but its five pages are the product of no fewer than thirty-two pages of sketches; no other work of his approaches this proportion.

Among the folk texts he brought with him from Russia he discovered several versions of a tale about how various farmyard animals outwit a marauding fox. From them he prepared a text for a short dramatic work, to be mimed and danced by acrobats. While he was working on it the Princesse de Polignac, a wealthy American (née Winnaretta Singer, heiress to the Singer sewing machine fortune), asked him for a work that a small group of musicians could perform in her drawing-room. Her request crystallized the work in progress into the 'burlesque story to be sung and acted', *Renard*. The performance never took place – the Princess may have intended the commission as a way of helping Stravinsky financially without embarrassing him – but it gave him a means of expanding his new 'Russian' style to a time-scale greater than the miniatures that he had already written, and to explore in the wake of his dissatisfaction with *The Nightingale* a new form of musical drama.

As he began working on *Renard* he realized that his text was too short, and he decided to repeat the episode of the cock being lured from his perch by the fox, who is disguised as a nun. This anti-realism is an inherent part of the work, in which the four vocal soloists do not take part in the action and are not identified with individual characters. The drama is further 'recessed' from the audience by an opening and closing march during which the performers enter and leave the hall. Their appeal at the end for money emphasizes the fact that they are performers, not characters. The text is more concerned with word-play and sheer nonsense than with narrative. Word-play becomes rhythmic play in Stravinsky's setting, where short, syncopated melodic cells are juggled with the greatest virtuosity, alternating with passages of stricter rhythm, both scored with raucous vividness for an orchestra of fifteen players.

In all these respects *Renard* is a crucial work in Stravinsky's output, and crucial to its sound-world was the discovery of a new sonority, or rather the re-discovery of an old one. One night in Geneva he dined with his friend the conductor Ernest Ansermet. The music in the restaurant was provided by Aladár Rácz, a performer on the Hungarian cimbalom or dulcimer, a zither-like instrument whose strings are not plucked, but struck with spoon-shaped sticks, their ends padded with wool. Stravinsky was entranced by its percussive yet resonant sound, both for its own sake and for its resemblance to the smaller and quieter Russian dulcimer, the *gusli* (one of *Renard*'s jokes is that the *gusli* is played by the cloven-hoofed goat). He rapidly questioned Rácz about its qualities, tried it himself and ended by buying his own cimbalom and learning to play it. For some while he actually composed at it instead of the piano, and its sonority pervades not only the two works in which he incorporated a cimbalom, *Renard* and *Ragtime*, but other pieces of this period and after, not least the harsh crooning of 'Sektanskaya', whose awkward piano accompaniment reveals that it was conceived for the cimbalom.

The cimbalom was central to the protracted conception of *Les Noces*, which Stravinsky carried around in his head for a decade, imagining it clearly but unable to bring it into focus. He began making musical sketches while compiling the text, in 1913, and envisaged scoring it for an extremely large orchestra incorporating folk instruments (including guitars and *gusli*, he hoped, though the latter instrument was almost obsolete). He had in mind a quite realistic portrayal of a Russian peasant wedding, with detailed characterization of the participants and a good deal of 'plot' in the form of precisely described action. As his conception moved, with the help of *Renard*, in the direction of a more stylized treatment (in Stravinsky's words 'to present rather than to describe') so the paraphernalia of the symphony orchestra with, in the theatre, its overtones of late nineteenth-century 'realist' opera, became increasingly inappropriate. He tried to stylize the orchestra itself, by placing it on stage with the singers and dancers, its individual groups physically separated. The orchestra now included cimbalom, piano and harpsichord, and part of the string force allied itself to their plucked sonority by playing *pizzicato* throughout. His next idea was a band incorporating two cimbaloms, mechanical piano and

Renard (1922): costume
design for the title-role by
Mikhail Larionov

Renard: a preliminary
drawing (1921)
by Mikhail Larionov

harmonium; he also considered the combination of mechanical pianos with brass instruments. This obsession with player pianos (during the 1920s he transcribed many of his works on to piano rolls) reflects, according to his Swiss friend the writer C. F. Ramuz, who prepared the French translation of *Les Noces* in collaboration with the composer, the intention of simulating the Orchestrion, the coin-in-the-slot mechanical instrument that had been widespread throughout Europe since the early nineteenth century, and which might indeed have provided music for the dancing at a Russian peasant wedding of the type Stravinsky had in mind.

In the end he 'suddenly realized' that an ensemble of four pianos and percussion would meet all his musical and dramatic needs: 'It would be at the same time perfectly homogeneous, perfectly impersonal, and perfectly mechanical.' As the scenario of the work was transformed from a realistic description of a peasant wedding to a ritualized abstract of one, an anthology of folk customs and proverbial sayings, the sound in Stravinsky's head changed from that of a *gusli*-dominated village band to a more hieratic one centred around

Renard: the Cat, the Goat and the Cockerel; a scene from the 1929 revival

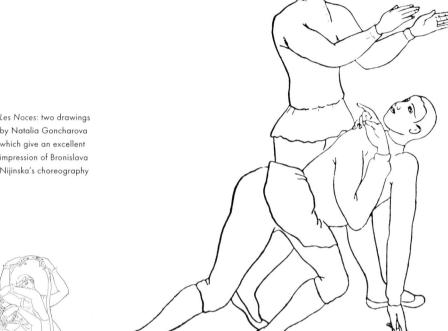

Les Noces: two drawings by Natalia Goncharova which give an excellent impression of Bronislava Nijinska's choreography

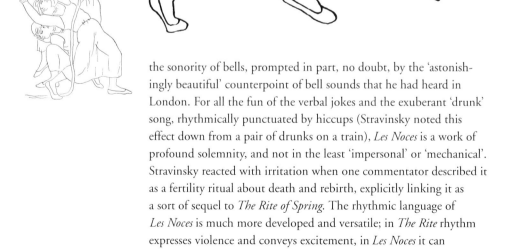

the sonority of bells, prompted in part, no doubt, by the 'astonishingly beautiful' counterpoint of bell sounds that he had heard in London. For all the fun of the verbal jokes and the exuberant 'drunk' song, rhythmically punctuated by hiccups (Stravinsky noted this effect down from a pair of drunks on a train), *Les Noces* is a work of profound solemnity, and not in the least 'impersonal' or 'mechanical'. Stravinsky reacted with irritation when one commentator described it as a fertility ritual about death and rebirth, explicitly linking it as a sort of sequel to *The Rite of Spring*. The rhythmic language of *Les Noces* is much more developed and versatile; in *The Rite* rhythm expresses violence and conveys excitement, in *Les Noces* it can

Ballets Russes poster, 1923:
with the première of Les
Noces half of Diaghilev's
repertoire was danced to
music by Stravinsky

encompass innocent joy, gravity, lamentation, above all grace. It
would be too easy to see *Les Noces* as a Christian pendant to *The Rite*,
despite its strong overtones of Orthodox chant. But like its
predecessor it is a rite, and has a much clearer view of ritual-as-drama.
Around this time Stravinsky was repelled by a suggestion from
Diaghilev that he write a setting of the Russian Orthodox Mass, to be
mounted as a stage spectacle with vestments and icons.

Les Noces is a more intensely Russian work than *The Rite of Spring*.
The entire work stems from the melodic implications of song and
spoken Russian, and from the style explored in the works of
Stravinsky's 'Russian phase'. In the clear brilliance of its sound-world,
the motoric rhythms of its syllabic word-setting, its refinement of
all *The Rite*'s discoveries freed of that work's extravagant resources, it
prepared a way for the 'international' language of Stravinsky's
middle years.

Although conceived during his first years of exile, it did not
achieve final form and performance (in Paris in 1923) until long after
his exile had become definitive. The war years produced another work

'The kindest of men ... and the liveliest': Stravinsky's sketch of his collaborator on *The Soldier's Tale*, C. F. Ramuz.

that, while clearly related to *Renard* and *Les Noces* in its dramaturgy and use of Russian folk tales, represents a later stage on the path from a Russian style to a cosmopolitan one. In Switzerland Stravinsky was friendly with a group of artists all of whom were feeling the pinch of curtailed artistic activity during wartime. When he finished the short score of *Les Noces*, content to leave the definitive instrumentation until there should be some prospect of performing it, he and C. F. Ramuz had the idea of a short dramatic entertainment, as simple to stage as possible, that could be toured to small towns without theatres as well as to cities, even performed in the open air. They agreed also

Natalia Goncharova's
design for scene 4 of *Les
Noces* (1923), showing two
of the four pianos that
appeared on stage with the
dancers and contributed to
the overall colour scheme of
black and brown

that the music should be independent of the drama, thus detachable for separate performance. Stravinsky introduced Ramuz to a folk tale from one of the collections he had brought from Russia, about a soldier who sells his soul (in the form of a fiddle) to the devil, and the two set to work.

Stravinsky chose his instrumental group with great care, to provide the maximum contrast of sonority with the minimum number of players: clarinet and bassoon, cornet and trombone, percussion, double bass and violin. The latter, of course, because of its importance in the story, and Stravinsky had already dreamed a fragment of melody for it: in the dream a gipsy-woman sat by the side of the road playing over and over again a tiny melodic figure which happens to be a decorated variant of the 'Dies irae' chant from the Mass for the Dead. The percussion is important too, partly because it articulates Stravinsky's by now fluent rhythmic virtuosity, partly because of its association (as the violin characterizes the Soldier) with the Devil – at the end, the Devil dances in triumph to the sound of drums alone. Percussion is also essential to Stravinsky's evocation in this score of jazz: the awakening of the Princess from a magic slumber and her growing joy are portrayed by a sequence of dances: a languorous tango, a sprightly waltz and an exuberant ragtime.

Stravinsky had only recently encountered jazz, from printed copies brought back from the USA by Ernest Ansermet. Its syncopated rhythm interested him, as an addition to his armoury of rhythmic resource, and he seems to have regarded his use of it as a 'final break with the Russian orchestral school'. *The Soldier's Tale* may represent a recognition of his final break with Russia itself, with its deliberate anthology of Western dances and its no less deliberate 'deRussification' of the folk tale (he and Ramuz were insistent that the drama be applicable to any place and to any time, including the present; at the first performance the Soldier wore the uniform of a private in the Swiss army).

Stravinsky had at first welcomed the 1917 Revolution. He had greeted its predecessor, the abortive uprising of 1905, with enthusiasm, and in 1914 told the French novelist Romain Rolland that the World War would end in a revolution which would supplant the Romanov dynasty and form a 'United States of Russia'. He seems to have seen Russia as a potentially great culture (in his conversation

Opposite, asked to design a cover for Stravinsky's piano transcription of *Ragtime*, 1919, Picasso offered three for Stravinsky to choose from, all formed from a single unbroken line.

Picasso and Stravinsky, a
caricature by Jean Cocteau;
it was originally captioned
'After the revival of *The
Rite* and *Parade*, Picasso
comforts Stravinsky. He has
drunk too much vodka'.

with Rolland he spoke of 'a beautiful and mighty country, pregnant
with embryos of new ideas'), but one forcibly withheld from development by the corrupt and reactionary tsarist regime. Immediately
after the 'Liberal Revolution' of March 1917 he wrote to his mother
and surviving elder brother, 'All my thoughts are with you in these
unforgettable days of happiness that are sweeping across our dear,
liberated Russia.' He sincerely wanted a new Russia, but there is not
a word in his published writings or correspondence to suggest that he
sympathized with or even understood communism.

His disillusion was swift. He never did learn what had become of
his property at Ustilug, but many years later the conductor Gennadi
Rozhdestvensky found, on a bookstall in Moscow, the title-page
only of Book II of Debussy's *Préludes*, inscribed by the composer 'to
entertain my friend Igor Stravinsky'. It seems likely that his library
and other effects, put in store by his cousins during World War II,
were looted and destroyed. The loss of Ustilug, the place where he
had been happiest, was undoubtedly the main reason for Stravinsky's
hostility to the new regime in Russia.

The war years had not completely put a stop to his travels in
Western Europe and his transformation into a Western cosmopolite.
Diaghilev managed to re-establish his company in 1916. It did not
return to Paris until late in the war, spending long periods touring in
the USA, but Stravinsky rejoined his friends for seasons in Madrid
and in Rome. Spain entranced him, and evocations of it began
appearing in his music (the Royal March in *The Soldier's Tale* is a
street-band *paso doble* of a type he enjoyed hearing in Madrid). In
Rome he met Pablo Picasso, who became a close friend. Because
of the Revolution, Diaghilev's company could no longer use the
Imperial Russian national anthem; Stravinsky made an arrangement
of the *Song of the Volga Boatmen* instead, and Picasso painted a red
banner, symbolic of the Revolution, on the cover of the manuscript.

Stravinsky and Picasso followed the company to Naples, which
they explored together, one evening attending a *commedia dell'arte*
performance at which, Stravinsky said, 'The Pulcinella was a great
drunken lout whose every gesture, and probably every word if I had

Diaghilev's team, 1915.
Standing: Léonide Massine,
Mikhail Larionov, Léon
Bakst; seated: Natalia
Goncharova, Stravinsky

understood, was obscene.' When Diaghilev suggested two years later that he write a ballet on just such a *commedia dell'arte* subject, based on music by Pergolesi, Stravinsky 'thought he must be deranged'. The suggestion, put to the composer of *The Rite of Spring* who was wrestling with the problems of *Les Noces*, must have seemed odd if not cynical. Ballet scores 'after' a composer of the past, seasoning the palatably familiar with the spice of modern orchestration, were proving popular with the public, especially – Diaghilev had a shrewd eye for his new Italian audience – when the composers concerned were Italian. Diaghilev had already had successes with *La Boutique fantasque* (music by Rossini, expertly re-scored by Respighi) and with *The Good-Humoured Ladies* (for which the Italian composer Vincenzo Tommasini orchestrated a sequence of harpsichord sonatas by Domenico Scarlatti). When Stravinsky eventually accepted the commission, having in the meanwhile 'fallen in love' (his phrase) with Pergolesi's music, some of his admirers were disconcerted by *his* apparent cynicism. *Pulcinella*, his ballet 'after Pergolesi', was the first work of an entire new phase, preoccupied with an evocation of the musical past and thus, it seemed, a turning away from the forward-moving frontier of modernism.

Stravinsky's 'arrangements' of Pergolesi (in fact many of the originals on which he worked have proved to be by other eighteenth-century composers) appear deceptively modest: for the most part he leaves the melodies and their harmonies intact, and only occasionally introduces elements of his own newly developed rhythmic language. But by vivid instrumental colouring and piquant additions to the harmony he creates a score which is genuinely both Pergolesi and Stravinsky. He must have noticed with pleasure that 'Pergolesi's' word-setting takes as liberal an attitude to the stresses of spoken Italian as his own recent vocal works had to Russian. One of the most 'Stravinskian' sounds in the piece, the exuberantly lurching duet for trombone and double bass, was originally scored (hardly less eccentrically in the 1730s) for cello and double bass. Stravinsky, aware that he could not 'forge' Pergolesi, set out instead to 'repeat him in my own accent'. But 'repeating' Pergolesi inevitably involved repeating his eighteenth-century harmonic formulae and the syntax, the conventional formal structures that they articulate. They were very remote from Stravinsky's own practice, but he seems to have enjoyed

Opposite, Pulcinella and Harlequin: Picasso continues to explore the *commedia dell'arte* theme of his collaboration with Stravinsky in a drawing made three months after the première of *Pulcinella*.

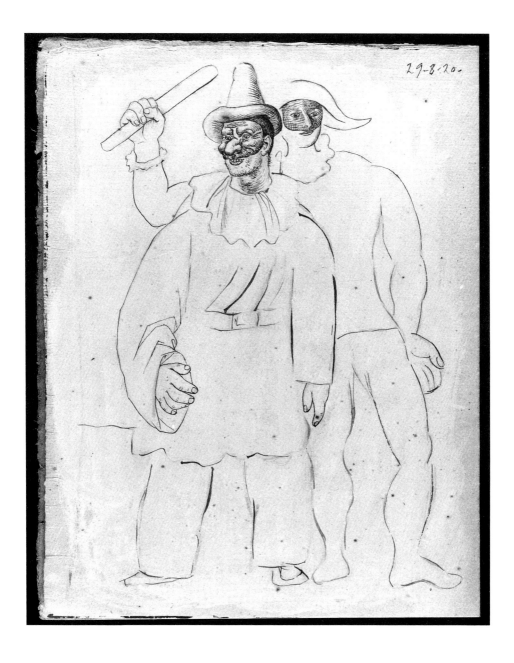

Pimpinella and Pulcinella:
two costume designs
by Picasso

Picasso's costume designs
translated to the stage:
Lydia Lopokova and
Leon Woizikovsky as
Pimpinella and Pulcinella,
London 1923

sometimes using them, sometimes contradicting them with elements
from his own language.

Two works that Stravinsky began immediately after the war but
did not finish until after *Pulcinella* give an interesting sidelight on
why he abandoned his Russian manner. The Concertino for String
Quartet is an obvious development and extension of the Three
Pieces for the same medium that had heralded the 'Russian phase'.
The Symphonies of Wind Instruments, which had their origin in a
commission from a French musical magazine for a short piano piece
in memory of Debussy (who died during the last year of the war) are
audibly related, in their intermittent use of folk-like material, to the
Russian works in general and, in their recurrent bell-like pealings, to
Les Noces in particular. Although the Concertino and the Symphonies
sound dissimilar, scored as they are for four solo strings and for a
large wind band of twenty-three players respectively, they have many
features in common, in particular an attempt to weld the elements
of Stravinsky's language as it had matured so far into a satisfyingly

extended structure (of about six and twelve minutes respectively) in
a purely instrumental work, without a verbal or dramatic framework.
Both proceed by abrupt juxtaposition of strongly dissimilar material;
ideas may be repeated, varied, even changed, but 'development', in
the sense in which it had been understood in Western music for
generations, even in the brief and very simple structures of Pergolesi,
takes place hardly at all. The Symphonies in particular – their
cross-cut chimings, song-fragments, punched chords and wailing,
which reach with magical inevitability the stoic chorale that is
Stravinsky's personal act of mourning for Debussy – have a powerful
but almost inexplicable impetus and unity.

It is hard to say whether for personal as well as musical reasons
Stravinsky felt that it was time to bring his 'Russian phase' to an end,
or whether his work on the Concertino and the Symphonies, interrupted by the exercise of 'repeating' Pergolesi in his own voice,
led him to examine other musical forms in which his music might
expand. It is also hard to separate his adoption in the years that
followed of certain aspects of the music of the past from his acknowledged tendency to 'kleptomania'. (Taxed with having 'borrowed'
from Rossini in a later ballet he is said to have replied 'To Hell! I
stole Rossini'.) In *Petrushka* he had 'stolen', apart from a number of
traditional melodies (and the unfortunately not traditional 'She Had
a Wooden Leg'), a Viennese waltz by Josef Lanner – just the thing
for a wooden-headed puppet ballerina. The waltz in *The Soldier's
Tale* is another theft from Lanner or perhaps Waldteufel, only this
time Stravinsky wrote it himself: he stole the manner rather than
the matter.

This tendency is perhaps closer to a game with masks than to
kleptomania. Another group of short pieces from this period, little
studied because they seem to contain little material for study, cast an
interesting light on Stravinsky's assumption of 'manners' or masks.
All of them are in fact teaching pieces for children, but the dedi-
cations of the first group, the Three Easy Pieces for Piano Duet,
indicate that their original function was to amuse grown-ups as well.
A March, dedicated to his friend the Italian composer Alfredo
Casella, plays a witty game with all those elements that spell 'military
music' (including an apparent half-quotation from Schubert).
A Waltz pays the sincerest and most affectionate of homages to its

Stravinsky with Léonide Massine, Lausanne, 1915. At this time Diaghilev was still hoping that Stravinsky would soon finish *Les Noces*, and that Massine would choreograph it. In fact *Les Noces* was not completed until 1923; Stravinsky and Massine collaborated on the revised production of *The Rite of Spring* and on *The Song of the Nightingale*, both in 1920.

dedicatee, Erik Satie, including his fondness for the clichés of popular music; there is a distinct hint, in the rapid repeated notes and ornaments for the more gifted of the two pianists (in each piece the other has only a simple repeated pattern) of Stravinsky's liking for the mechanical piano. The final Polka also recalls Satie, but was written for and is a good-natured caricature of Diaghilev, portrayed as a whip-wielding circus ring-master.

The second series of Five Easy Pieces was written in 1916/17 for the two older Stravinsky children, Theodore and Lyudmila (Mika), who were now taking piano lessons. Here the 'easy' melody part is given prominence, all the more difficult passages being given to the second player (Stravinsky himself) at the left-hand end of the keyboard. The opening Andante is a poised and beautiful melody so like Satie that it might be by him, as though Stravinsky were intrigued to find the secret of the older man's lucid simplicity. There follow an Española (memories of the trip to Madrid, where he had heard not only *paso dobles* but coin-in-the-slot mechanical pianos in cafés), a Balalaika (Stravinsky's own favourite, and a link with the 'Russian' miniatures, their melodies often built from rather few notes), a Napoletana (a postcard from Italy this time, with a direct quotation from the verse, not the chorus, of Luigi Denza's 'Funiculì, funiculà') and a lively French circus Galop.

In all of these pieces Stravinsky is not only humorously or affectionately evoking an 'alien' style, he is necessarily adopting features of its grammar, while making entirely personal use of them. The Waltz from the earlier set, for example, has the expected, banal 'one-two-three' accompaniment, but the practical need to repeat it without any variation at all brings it very close to the obstinate 'motor' rhythms that were already a hallmark of Stravinsky's idiom, and would soon become still more marked. The ornate melody line, derived with elegant wit from the mechanical roulades of the street piano (the so-called barrel-organ), has a close kinship with the florid, quasi-Baroque figurations that were soon to give rise to the term 'neo-classical'.

4

Stravinsky, c. 1920

In classical dancing I see the triumph of studied conception over vagueness, of the rule over the arbitrary, of order over the haphazard. I am thus brought face to face with the eternal conflict in art between the Apollonian and the Dionysian principles.

Stravinsky: *Chronicles of my Life*

A Cosmopolitan in Paris 1920–39

Despite the many friends that he had made in Switzerland Stravinsky found it too far, once the war was over, from the great centres of musical performance. Perhaps he also felt a certain nostalgia for cities, after several years in the countryside of the Vaud. An exile from the Italianate city of St Petersburg, his first thought was to live in Rome. When that idea came to nothing he returned to France, which was to remain his home for nearly twenty years.

Paris was once again a city of artistic ferment, and Diaghilev's company had returned there. Many of Stravinsky's pre-war friends were there to welcome him back: Ravel, Cocteau, Satie and others, as well as more recent acquaintances like Picasso and a whole generation of younger composers for whom Stravinsky, not yet forty himself, was an admired and acknowledged leader. When the very young Francis Poulenc first saw Stravinsky, quite unexpectedly, 'I thought it was God Himself ... I often ask myself: "If Stravinsky had not existed, would I have written music?" Which means that I consider myself ... a spiritual son of Stravinsky.' No member of the group of composers who were soon bracketed together as 'Les Six' (Poulenc, Georges Auric, Louis Durey, Arthur Honegger, Darius Milhaud and Germaine Tailleferre) escaped Stravinsky's influence, and there was soon widespread talk of 'Stravinsky's school'.

Stravinsky encountered many of the leading writers, artists and musicians of the day either through their mutual association with Diaghilev (in this way, for example, he met Reynaldo Hahn, and through him Marcel Proust) or in such salons as those of the Princesse de Polignac, of Cyprien ('Cipa') and Ida Godebski and of Cipa Godebski's half-sister Marie ('Misia'), who successively married Thadée Natanson (co-founder of the immensely influential literary journal *La Revue Blanche*), Alfred Edwards (proprietor of *Le Matin*) and the Catalan painter Jose-Maria Sert. Regular visitors at the Godebskis' or at Misia Sert's (as she is usually known, having re-married her third husband after the death of his second wife for

Madrid, 1921 (left to right): Robert Delaunay, Boris Kochno, Stravinsky, Sonia Delaunay, Diaghilev, Manuel de Falla, Randolfo Barocchi (one of Diaghilev's backers for his seasons in Italy)

Following page, Léopold Survage's set design for the first production of *Mavra* (1922); the tiny one room set was almost lost on the vast stage of the Paris Opéra.

whom he divorced her) included Cocteau, André Gide, Paul Valéry and many composers: Ravel, Falla, Satie and several members of 'Les Six'.

There was however no 'Stravinsky circle' in Paris, firstly because although he moved to France in 1920 he had no permanent home in Paris until 1934. For the sake of his wife's health he needed to make his home in a mild climate. The 1920s and 1930s were also a period during which his private and professional life involved him in a vast amount of travelling; even if his home had been in the French capital he would have been able to spend only limited periods there. His change of musical direction since his last overwhelming impact on Paris with *The Rite of Spring* also ensured that he would soon be attacked as often by the avant garde as by the old guard.

His first three post-war offerings to the Paris public must have confused them. *Pulcinella*, with its pungently colourful evocation of the eighteenth century, was a great success with audiences, though its engagement with the past and detachment from the present disconcerted some critics. It was followed by the one-act opera *Mavra*, and when that in its turn was succeeded by *Les Noces*, in conception earlier than *Pulcinella* or *Mavra*, it seemed that Stravinsky was changing his style with arbitrary abruptness.

Stravinsky described *Pulcinella* as 'my discovery of the past, the epiphany through which the whole of my late work became possible'. Although *Mavra*'s Russian text, drawn from a story by Pushkin, might suggest a return to the 'Russian phase' it continues *Pulcinella*'s exploration of the past, specifically that of Glinka. Since Glinka was not only the father of Russian music but the translator into Russian of various Western musical conventions (notably the patterned accompaniment figures and florid vocal lines of early nineteenth-century Italian opera) these too are refracted through Stravinsky's wittily distorting lens. The 'till-ready' accompaniments, florid emotions and ornate coloratura of Stravinsky's 'originals' are affectionately parodied, rhythmically dislocated and seasoned with deliberately anachronistic ragtime. Perhaps most disconcerting of all for a work intended as an artistic manifesto, its plot is a comedy of featherweight slightness. The heroine Parasha disguises her soldier-lover as a woman and tricks her mother into engaging 'her' as a cook. The little opera, playing for less than half an hour, is dedicated 'to the memory of Pushkin, Glinka and Tchaikovsky'. The polemical intention behind this is one reason for the work's dismal failure at its Paris première in 1922; another was the presentation of this diminutive farce in the vast space of the Paris Opéra.

For French aesthetes, schooled by Debussy and Diaghilev himself, the great Russian composers were Mussorgsky and the nationalists, to whom Stravinsky himself had once seemed like a forward-looking successor. Stravinsky, while not relinquishing an admiration for Mussorgsky, now stepped forward and, in the dedication of *Mavra* and a number of public statements, dismissed 'picturesque' nationalism and asserted the superiority of the 'Italo-Slav' Glinka, then little known outside Russia, and of Tchaikovsky, a composer deeply unfashionable among Western intellectuals. Stravinsky's next composition, the Octet, a work of brilliant, glancing wit, a twentieth-century divertimento, was equipped with a solemn apologia of its own: 'My Octet is a musical object. This object has a form and that form is influenced by the musical matter with which it is composed. The differences of matter determine the differences of form. One does not do the same with marble that one does with stone.' This says nothing about the feigned 'classical' sonata form of the first movement or the destabilized Bach-plus-jazz of the finale, and nothing at all about the work's geniality.

Opposite, poster advertising the première of Stravinsky's Octet

THEATRE NATIONAL
OPÉRA

JEUDI 18 OCTOBRE 1923

RIDEAU à **21** heures

Deuxième Concert Symphonique
(4me Saison, Première Série)

SERGE KOUSSEVITZKY

Avec le concours de MM.

I. STRAVINSKY et M. DARRIEUX (Violon)

PROGRAMME

1) **SYMPHONIE** en *Ré majeur* (1re audition) . POLACI
2) **OCTETT** pour instrument à vent (1re audition) . I. STRAVINSKY
sous la direction de l'**AUTEUR**
3) **CONCERTO** p' violon et orchestre (1re audition). S. PROKOFIEFF
Violon-solo : **M. DARRIEUX**
4) **3me SYMPHONIE** (Eroica) . . . . BEETHOVEN

Orchestre de 100 exécutants, sous la direction de

M. SERGE KOUSSEVITZKY

La Location est ouverte à l'OPÉRA et chez M. DURAND, 4, place de la Madeleine

Le **3me Concert Koussevitzky** aura lieu le **Jeudi 25 Octobre 1923**, à **21** heures

Vendredi **19** Octobre, **THAIS**

Samedi **20** Octobre, **SAMSON ET DALILA — COPPELIA**

Dimanche **21** Octobre
En Matinée : **ROMÉO** et **JULIETTE** — *En Soirée :* **HÉRODIADE**

Lundi **22** Octobre, **LOHENGRIN**

Mercredi **24** Octobre, **LA DAMNATION DE FAUST**

Bureau de Location de 11 h. à 17 h. 30, dans le bâtiment de l'Opéra, rue Auber

Soe du Pune Artistique, Industrielle et Commerciale, 53, rue du Château-d'Eau (Nord 85-90)   Imp. ALBERT PIC. 3b — Paris

In one sense Stravinsky had become a Frenchman overnight. The public espousal of attitudes, the propagation and debate of cultural dogmas and manifestos, was typical of the artistic life of Paris. From this point on, culminating in the publication in the mid-1930s of his autobiography *Chronicles of my Life* and of his Harvard lectures (1939/40) on 'The Poetics of Music', Stravinsky made numerous pronouncements on his own music and on musical aesthetics in general. Whenever a creative artist makes statements of this kind they are likely to contain an element of self-justification, even an attempt to explain to themselves the course they have taken.

Discussion of Stravinsky's music of this period has concentrated on its most obvious attribute, described by the convenient but insufficient term 'neo-classicism'. Stravinsky himself disliked the word, saying that it meant 'absolutely nothing'. One of his oracular statements (the italics are Stravinsky's) was pungently provocative: 'I consider that music is, by its very nature, essentially powerless to *express* anything at all, whether a feeling, an attitude of mind, a psychological mood, a phenomenon of nature, etc. *Expression* has never been an inherent property of music. That is by no means the purpose of its existence.' The assumption behind the term 'neo-classical' is that Stravinsky was, in another frequently repeated phrase, going 'back to Bach' in search of formal perfection coupled with, taking his celebrated utterance at face value, a chilly detachment from emotion. Both the term 'neo-classical' and Stravinsky's statement are a positive hindrance to describing, let alone appreciating, the masterpieces of this period, in which the stylistic references are not exclusively or even primarily to the 'classical' eighteenth century, and which are profoundly and surely intentionally expressive.

At this point it should be said that most of Stravinsky's major aesthetic statements were made through intermediaries. Several influential and still often-quoted articles from the 1920s were written by the expatriate Russian musician Arthur Lourié, who for some while acted as Stravinsky's musical assistant, reading proofs for him and preparing piano reductions. How far his articles were written at Stravinsky's behest and with his assistance, how far Lourié may have helped Stravinsky with articles under his own name, is hard to establish. Stravinsky's religious views, too, seem to owe something to Lourié, who was an enthusiastic follower of the French religious philosopher Jacques Maritain. But the two quarrelled in the 1930s (Lourié seems to have intrigued in some way against Stravinsky's future second wife) and his name became so unmentionable in the Stravinsky household that even the closest musical associate of his later years, his 'surrogate son' Robert Craft, felt unable to question him about this shadowy figure.

Stravinsky's *Chronicles* were written in collaboration with his friend Walter Nouvel, Diaghilev's company secretary and business manager. The Harvard lectures, delivered in French, were largely written by the French composer Roland-Manuel, using an outline by Stravinsky and transcriptions of interviews. His later books were based on transcribed conversations, conducted with and edited by Robert Craft. All these appeared with Stravinsky's authority (in the case of the *Chronicles* and the lectures without any public acknowledgement of collaboration), but the intervention of another tone of voice should warn us against assuming that the words chosen are precisely those that he would have used. Stravinsky himself was aware of the discrepancy of language between the books, and wanted the volume published as '*Conversations with Stravinsky* by Igor Stravinsky and Robert Craft' to appear as '*Conversations with Stravinsky* by Robert Craft'. How far these close friends of his youth, middle and old age put words into Stravinsky's mouth (that he was content to appear to utter), how far his changing opinions and attitudes dictated his choice of partner in their propagation is hard to determine.

Stravinsky was conscious of his position as a leading figure in modern music. He acknowledged that the end of the 'Russian phase' was one of the two great crises of his creative life, the other being his later coming to terms with Schoenbergian serialism. Several works of this period, the most obvious being *Les Noces*, cost him great trouble to bring into focus, trouble that is minimized or passed over in his own commentaries. It seems likely that his published *obiter dicta* were intended as polemics to demonstrate that his new style had a coherent theory behind it. Although he scorned the 'neo-classical' label, his own writings and statements made the coining of that term almost inevitable, especially when the works contain obvious references to classical forms and phraseology.

The word 'references' is, however, important. Stravinsky's references to the past in his works of the three decades following *Les Noces*

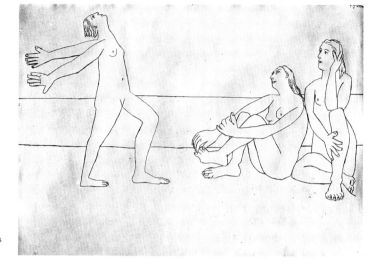

Picasso's 'neo-classicism': in this drawing of 1920 Picasso, still under the influence of his collaboration with Stravinsky and Diaghilev, looks forward to his monumental figure paintings of a few years later.

are innumerable: passages of Baroque-style florid ornament, textbook harmonic sequences and cadences, piano figurations strongly recalling Mozart. In no case is the style or period referred to evoked literally. A quasi-Baroque aria with distinctly Bachian ornaments will be underpinned, not by an accompaniment with a strong sense of motion between key-centres, as in Bach, but by an unchanging pattern or a characteristically Stravinskian play of rhythmic permutations. In movements ostensibly in classical sonata form, the contrasting ideas, their keys often rendered ambiguous by their own accompaniments, are not set in genuinely classical structural conflict but piquantly juxtaposed.

Stravinsky's neo-classicism is in fact in an important sense a continuation of those games with popular musical styles, those masks that he enjoyed trying on in the two sets of Easy Pieces for piano duet. Interestingly enough, in the 'sequel' to these, the set of eight little pieces for children that he wrote immediately after *Pulcinella* and called 'The Five Fingers' (*Les Cinq Doigts*), titles referring to style are almost entirely abandoned. The style referred to here is that of *Pulcinella* itself, and of Italianate classicism in general. When listening to the works of this period we are alternately reassured by references to the familiar past, then disconcerted by their contradictions and their instability, by the fact that context renders the familiar unfamiliar.

An affinity with the so-called neo-classical works of Picasso, Stravinsky's collaborator on *Pulcinella*, has often been noted but seldom discussed in detail. Picasso was much less given than Stravinsky to polemics, and explanations for his change of direction have varied widely, from his rediscovery of Cézanne, of Ingres or of Poussin; via the influence of working among dancers in the theatre (for Diaghilev) and the new domestic tranquillity that he found after marrying one of those dancers, Olga Khokhlova; to the malign bourgeois influence of Olga herself, who 'civilized' Picasso, taking him from his suburban home at Montrouge to a large apartment in the fashionable rue la Boétie, and saw to it that he moved in 'society'.

At Juan-les-Pins, 1925: Cocteau, Picasso, Stravinsky, Olga Picasso.

In Stravinsky's case argument has centred around his own aesthetic
statements, but it may well be that their time together in Italy
affected both artists equally deeply. Picasso, whose affinity with the
world of clowns and mountebanks was already marked, immediately
took the *commedia dell'arte* into his imaginative world. In Rome he
studied Raphael and Michelangelo with great attention. Stravinsky
recorded little of this period save that he and Picasso, arrested late
one evening for urinating against a wall in Naples, insisted that the
policeman take them to the opera house, where they were respectfully
released when theatre staff addressed them both as 'maestro'. But
he too may have 'recognized' the masked world of the *commedia
dell'arte* players. His next major work after *Pulcinella* was to be much
concerned with masks. And in Italy, in Rome especially, that city that
was always to remind him of St Petersburg, he must have noticed the
coexistence of a palimpsest of styles: an early Christian basilica behind
a Baroque façade, a nineteenth-century stock exchange built within
the columns of a temple to the deified Emperor Hadrian.

   Of his private life at this time Stravinsky understandably tells us
next to nothing. After leaving Switzerland he and his family first
stayed in Brittany for the summer of 1920, then moved for the winter

Left, Stravinsky in his Pleyel
studio, Paris 1924
Right, Vera Sudeikina at
the time of her first meeting
with Stravinsky

to the fashion designer Gabrielle ('Coco') Chanel's house near Paris. He and Chanel briefly became lovers, and Stravinsky's family was moved to Biarritz, ostensibly for the sake of his wife's deteriorating health. He had just agreed with the Pleyel company to transcribe all his major works for mechanical piano, and as part of the contract was provided with a furnished studio which he used as a *pied-à-terre* in Paris. When Chanel left him for a Russian Grand Duke, Stravinsky began a relationship with a night-club singer. In February 1921, while living with Chanel, he was introduced by Diaghilev to the strikingly attractive Vera Sudeikina.

Dulac on Bakst and Diaghileff.

A caricature (1921) by Edmond Dulac showing Prince Charming (Diaghilev) being led by the Good Fairy (Léon Bakst) to the Sleeping Princess. Financially it was the evil fairy Carabosse who led Diaghilev to the very threshold of the bankruptcy courts.

After two brief and unsuccessful early marriages Vera de Bosset had eloped with the painter Serge Sudeikin just before the war. She had studied music as a child, and attended ballet school despite being too tall for a career as a dancer because her ambition was to become an actress. In Russia she appeared with the famous Kamerny Theatre and in a number of films. She and her husband moved in literary circles, he having decorated the 'Stray Dog' cabaret in St Petersburg, frequented by Anna Akhmatova, Osip Mandelshtam and other poets. Sudeikin was bisexual (many years earlier he had been one of Diaghilev's lovers), and during his first marriage to Olga Glebova had had a long relationship with another member of the 'Stray Dog' circle, the poet Mikhail Kuzmin. Akhmatova, who used Glebova and Kuzmin as leading, if shadowy, characters in her great *Poem without a Hero*, was attracted to Sudeikin herself, and reproachfully wrote 'Bad girl!' on a silhouette profile of Vera that she made around the time of the elopement (many years later she sent it to Vera through their mutual friend Sir Isaiah Berlin). The third poem in Mandelshtam's *Tristia* sequence, in which 'the wife beloved by all' is depicted at her embroidery, was written for Vera. She explained the beautiful but mysterious opening image of the poem (of a stream of honey being poured so slowly that the hostess has time to say 'Here in sad Tauris where fate has led us we are by no means bored') by the fact that Mandelshtam called on the Sudeikins unexpectedly, when the only food they had in the house was bread and honey. 'Fate' was the Easter Revolution; 'Tauris' the Crimea, from where the Sudeikins escaped to Western Europe via Turkey.

In the autumn of 1921, by which time Stravinsky and Vera were already lovers (they later celebrated 14 July as their 'wedding anniversary'), Diaghilev cast her in the mimed role of the Queen in his spectacular London production of *The Sleeping Beauty*. Intended to establish the Ballets Russes on a firm financial footing it was so expensively mounted that, despite a run of over one hundred per-formances, it reduced Diaghilev to near-bankruptcy; his principal backer impounded the sets, making it impossible to recoup some of the losses by a revival elsewhere. Stravinsky joined the company for a while, to help with the musical rehearsals (he had orchestrated a couple of numbers cut by Tchaikovsky before the first production, which Diaghilev wanted to reinstate) and to be with Vera. Virtually everyone who met and wrote about the couple remark on their obvious devotion to each other and the extreme physical contrast between them: he, the older by six years, unusually short for a man (five feet, two inches), wirily thin, earnest, bespectacled, intense, some might say ugly; she rather tall for a woman (five feet, seven inches), softly ample of figure, relaxed, laughing, beautiful. By the beginning of 1922 a triangular relationship had developed which was to last until Catherine Stravinsky's death seventeen years later. Vera became his second wife, and he her fourth husband, only in 1940.

Within a short while he told Catherine what had happened, saying that he could not live without Vera. He expected the two women to accept the situation and each other. They did become friends, though not without jealousy on Catherine's part. Vera left Sudeikin soon after her relationship with Stravinsky began. She had established a successful career designing and making theatrical costumes – for Diaghilev among others – as well as running a shop selling fashion accessories and another specializing in artificial flowers. All these and her home were in Paris, while Stravinsky's family lived first in Biarritz, then in Nice and near Grenoble, involving him in frequent travel between the two women.

The relationship was both widely known about and officially secret for many years, largely because Stravinsky feared that his mother might hear of it. She had stayed in Russia after the Revolution – when the Soviet state appropriated her husband's library she was appointed its curator – and was able to leave only in late 1922, proving immediately on her arrival that her ability to 'torment' her son had not diminished. An acquaintance describes her as reducing Stravinsky almost to tears by scolding him for not liking the music of her own idol, Skryabin ('There you go again, Igor, just the same as ever, criticizing your betters!'). Not surprisingly, he sent her to join his wife and children in Biarritz. Despite the occasional flash of suspicion she never learned of her son's relationship with Vera.

His emotional life was further complicated by a return to religion. His wife was, or at all events became during her long illness, deeply devout, and her letters to him are full of references to prayer, church-going and devotion to the saints; most are headed with a cross. Stravinsky himself officially returned to the Orthodox faith in 1926, regularly confessing and receiving communion, and at home keeping a candle burning in front of an icon of the Virgin. His confessor, the Orthodox priest Father Nicolas, became the Stravinsky family's 'chaplain' for five years.

Another and more embarrassing fact revealed in Catherine Stravinsky's letters to her husband is his closeness with money. She had to remind him to pay bills, even to beg for money for herself and her mother-in-law. It has to be said that the expenses of the household must have been considerable: the invalid woman, the elderly mother and four young children were looked after by up to five servants, and for several years Stravinsky also took responsibility for the expenses of his wife's sister's family, the Beliankins, who had recently arrived as refugees from Russia. But this generosity, which also extended to other needy friends and relatives, was combined with a degree of personal extravagance. Stravinsky had the small man's dapper neatness, combined in his case with a dandyish observance of fashion and a connoisseur's taste for food and wine. Alongside this went an almost miserly caution over small sums of money. Throughout his life he kept precise details of travelling and other expenses (in America, he meticulously recorded ten cents given to a beggar); he was a good deal better at remembering the debts of others than his own, and had a shrewd eye for petty economies. Even late in life, after the assassination of President Kennedy, he had to be persuaded not to send his telegram of condolence by the cheaper night rate.

The insecurities of the war years were by no means over. Diaghilev's frequent financial crises made it unwise for Stravinsky ever again to devote, as he had done in the years immediately before the war, most of his efforts to works for the Ballets Russes. After the completion of *Mavra* he turned to instrumental music for concert performance, first the Octet for Wind Instruments, then a Piano Concerto. Both were performed, in October 1923 and May 1924 respectively, at concerts promoted in Paris by the conductor Serge Koussevitzky. In 1921 Koussevitzky had premièred the Symphonies of Wind Instruments in London. The decision to play the work was made at the last moment, the parts arrived late, Stravinsky's work was not announced on the posters and in the event his austere ritual for wind instruments alone was placed at the end of a long concert of colourful music for full orchestra. To make matters worse

Following page, the Paris Opéra, the inappropriately grandiose setting that contributed to the failure of Stravinsky's diminutive one act opera Mavra (his Octet, The Song of the Nightingale and Pulcinella were also premièred there).

Koussevitzky did not re-arrange the platform for the Symphonies, leaving the handful of players in their original places at the rear of the stage, separated from him by a vast array of empty chairs. The work fell flat, and Stravinsky implied that it was to avoid a similar disaster that he resolved to conduct the first performance of the Octet himself. He had a bad attack of stage nerves and some listeners were amused by the sight of the diminutive composer conducting a group of eight players on the enormous stage of the Paris Opéra. He was satisfied with the performance, however, and intrigued by the problems of balance, projection and intonation that he had to solve; it was his first appearance in public as a conductor.

Koussevitzky then suggested that Stravinsky should play the solo part in the first performance of the Piano Concerto. He had returned to composing at the keyboard since deciding on the final scoring of *Les Noces*, and had recently made his virtuoso transcription of Three Dances from *Petrushka* for Artur Rubinstein, but he had not performed in public since leaving Russia. Early in 1924, with the Concerto still unfinished, he began to spend several hours a day polishing his technique and loosening his out-of-practice fingers. The première was a success, despite a moment of panic before the slow movement when his memory failed and he had to ask Koussevitzky to sing the first few notes. Stravinsky decided to retain exclusive performance rights in the work for five years. He realized that his fee for performing one of his own works (and he played the Concerto about forty times during those five years) would be greater than his royalty payment for it, and from this point on he began to travel quite widely fulfilling concert engagements. Over the next few years he added first a Piano Sonata and the Serenade in A, then the Capriccio for piano and orchestra, the *Duo concertant* for violin and piano (written for concerts with his friend the violinist Samuel Dushkin) and the Concerto for two solo pianos (for performance by Stravinsky and his son Soulima) to his repertory.

During the 1930s and 1940s his growing experience as a conductor first supplemented, then replaced, his activity as a pianist, but in the works written for his own instrument, the instrument which had always been and would remain central to his composing process, Stravinsky's development of the neo-classical language is fascinatingly summarized. His points of reference are very obvious

in the Concerto, with its quasi-Baroque slow introduction, the
Handelian solemnity of its slow movement and its running toccata
figurations that at times fuse jazz with the piano studies of Carl
Czerny, which Stravinsky had enjoyed practising while preparing
himself for the performance. So they are in the solo Sonata that he
wrote immediately thereafter, its extremely florid slow movement
sounding much more like Bach than the composer's own later, wry
description as 'Beethoven *frisé*'. The Rondoletto of the Serenade in
A, however, refracts the eighteenth century almost to the point of
abstraction. The Capriccio is a slighter work than the Concerto,
but also a more polished one, finding more elegant solutions to the
problem of combining piano and orchestra. The concerto is scored
for wind instruments, timpani and double basses only, but sounds
more massive than the full-orchestra Capriccio.

The two works for solo violin – the four-movement Concerto and
the rather awkwardly proportioned five-movement *Duo concertant* –
share something of the Capriccio's lighter manner and its overt
reference to a variety of musical styles. In the case of the Capriccio,
at least, Stravinsky acknowledged some of his sources, speaking of
Weber and Mendelssohn, 'the Beau Brummels of music', in relation
to the first movement, and of an element of 'Rumanian restaurant
music' in the second. In the Concerto for two solo pianos, the
masterpiece of this sequence, he was able to incorporate what he had
learned from a detailed study of Beethoven into a work that does not
quote or obviously refer to Beethoven at all. The overt references to
the past here are few, and never ironic, yet it includes Stravinsky's
closest approach to a genuinely classical sonata-form first movement.
There is a slow Notturno of poised lyrical grace (Stravinsky, quite
typically, denied that he was thinking of Chopin when choosing the
title, but of an eighteenth-century *Nachtmusik* or 'cassation') and a
set of variations and a concluding Prelude and Fugue that are
ingeniously linked by being based on the same theme, never actually
stated in its 'pure' form. The Concerto is the most 'abstract' of
Stravinsky's neo-classical works and, of those for instruments alone,
one of the most satisfying.

Stravinsky had for some years been wanting to write a large-scale
dramatic work. A life of St Francis of Assisi, picked up by chance at a
station bookstall, revealed that the saint was in the habit of praying in

Stravinsky recording
a piano roll in the Pleyel
studio in Paris, 1924

Provençal, his mother's language, Italian seeming to him too debased by everyday use for such a purpose. This suggested to Stravinsky the idea of composing a musical drama in a 'special' language, rather than his native Russian or adopted French. Latin, 'not dead but turned to stone', seemed to him ideal, and it was only after this decision was made that he began considering an appropriate plot; his eventual choice was Sophocles' *Oedipus Rex*. Both decisions, 'universal' plot and 'monumental' language, were intended to concentrate listeners' attention on the purely musical dramatization.

He had admired Jean Cocteau's version of Sophocles' *Antigone*, and asked him, in the greatest confidence, to draft a libretto. Secrecy was necessary since the work was intended as a tribute to Diaghilev to mark the twentieth anniversary of his work in the theatre. A text was eventually agreed and given to a priest, the Abbé Jean Daniélou, to translate into Latin. Stravinsky subtitled the work an 'opera–oratorio' and wanted it performed in a manner so formalized as to be static, the principal characters masked and motionless, the robed chorus in a single row, reading their parts, their faces hidden. In the event he was so late in completing the score that it was given in concert performance, in a double-bill with a staged *Firebird*, and suffered in consequence: the audience was puzzled and the critics chilly. Even Diaghilev remarked that it was a 'macabre gift'.

The subtitle of the work is precise: *Oedipus Rex* is an opera imbued with the attributes of oratorio by the monumental choral numbers and the tableau-like subdivision of the two acts into scenes by the narrator's spoken 'recitatives'. Stravinsky's references to Handelian oratorio and the crowd-choruses in Bach's Passions are obvious and have often been remarked. But the deft crispness and dry wit of the 'references' in his earlier neo-classical works are here replaced by a grandeur, a nobility of utterance that mark the first high point of Stravinsky's new style, while they may also reflect his renewed religious faith; it is no accident that *Oedipus Rex*, like *The Rite of Spring* and *Les Noces*, is a dramatic ritual. The operatic references, most evident in Jocasta's great aria, are to Italian opera, in particular to Verdi, for whose work Stravinsky never concealed his enthusiasm. Here again the affectionate mockery of operatic convention that was so much a part of *Mavra* has also vanished in favour of a compelling dramatic urgency. It is quite characteristic of Stravinsky, however, that he

Jean Cocteau's design for a mask for a 1952 Paris production of *Oedipus Rex*, in which Stravinsky conducted and Cocteau took the Narrator's part as well as designing and directing

Set by Ewald Dülberg for the famous 1929 production of *Oedipus Rex* at the Krolloper in Berlin, directed and conducted by Otto Klemperer

should have referred in his *Chronicles* to the 'anodyne and impersonal' nature of the models that he chose.

If *Oedipus Rex* can be seen as completing a triptych of stage rituals, with *The Rite of Spring* and *Les Noces*, it also belongs to a second triptych in company with Stravinsky's next two vocal works, the Symphony of Psalms and *Persephone*. The epically tragic *Oedipus Rex* and the vernally gracious *Persephone* complement one another on either side of his first major religious work. The Symphony of Psalms was commissioned by Serge Koussevitzky to celebrate the fiftieth anniversary of the Boston Symphony Orchestra (thus giving rise to the work's much ridiculed but quite sincerely intended superscription 'This Symphony, composed to the glory of GOD, is dedicated to the Boston Symphony Orchestra … '). Koussevitzky made no stipulations about the type of work; the decisions to use a chorus and a sacred text were Stravinsky's own. He had, he said, been carrying the idea of a choral symphony on psalm texts in his mind for some while.

It is a work of unification and culmination. In many respects, such as the very first vocal entry (an obsessive alternation of two notes) and the germinative idea from which the whole work sprang (a syncopated rhythm on a single note), it has obvious kinships with the works of the 'Russian phase'. Despite his recent experience with 'monumental' Latin, Stravinsky originally intended to set the psalm texts in Slavonic. It also takes neo-classicism a stage further, moving from oblique reference to classical forms to the literal adoption of one of the most classical of them all: double fugue. It is a work in which Stravinsky's practice and his stated theory are in obvious and inevitable conflict. The devout Stravinsky, writing a symphony 'to the glory of GOD' could hardly wish for it to do other than express his religious faith, yet 'music is, by its very nature, essentially powerless to express anything at all'. As his great double fugue, the first section of the second movement, comes to a quiet close, Stravinsky appears to contradict himself by marking the woodwind phrases to be played 'expressively' and 'sweetly'.

Yet this is not really a capitulation. Stravinsky's critique of 'expression' is in fact a defence of the autonomy of musical language, a resistance to saddling music with expressive epithets from other languages. Neo-classicism, beginning with works like *Mavra* and the Octet whose wit and exuberance may reflect relief at the discovery of

Alice Nikitina as
Terpsichore in George
Balanchine's 1928
production of *Apollo*

a fruitful new direction, grew to mastery in *Oedipus Rex* and the
Symphony of Psalms by the adaptation of Stravinsky's referential
technique to accord with the subject matter of an archetypal myth
and an act of worship.

The works surrounding these two masterpieces are often quasi-
religious or concerned with ritual. The two most crucial are the ballet
Apollo, originally entitled in Frenchified Greek 'Apollon Musagète'
('Apollo, leader of the Muses'), and the mélodrame *Persephone. Apollo*
is the first of Stravinsky's 'white' ballets, having no dramatic plot,
simply a ceremony in which the Muses pay homage to Apollo. It is
white also in scoring – strings only – and even in its appearance
on the page, with sparing use of sharps and flats, even of dissonances.
The expected references to the Baroque and Classical periods, to
Tchaikovsky and other sources are as a consequence very clearly
audible. But the ballet is 'classical' also in its evocation of the purest
language of classical dance. The work was commissioned by an
American patron, then offered to Diaghilev as well, so Stravinsky was
able to dictate the rudimentary plot and the character of each
individual dance number. According to Stravinsky himself, each
section is based on the metres of French classical verse. One
movement is headed by a quotation from the particular poem (by

Opposite, Svetlana
Beriosova in Frederick
Ashton's version of
Persephone for the Sadler's
Wells Ballet (now Royal
Ballet), London 1961

Boileau) that he had in mind. However this process worked
in detail it has given the score a rhythmic fluidity remarkable even
for Stravinsky.

Several writers, prompted by Stravinsky's own remarks, have
found it useful to speak of 'Apollonian' and 'Dionysian' elements
within his music. The latter – represented by the orgiastic *Rite of
Spring* and the vein of deep, 'pre-civilized' emotion that it taps –
needed, according to this interpretation, some formal, emotion-
restraining discipline, which Stravinsky found in the ordered world
of the eighteenth century. He explained the concept slightly
differently, casting light on his more often quoted denials of
'expression' in music. 'What is important for the lucid ordering of
the work', he wrote, 'is that all the Dionysian elements which set
the imagination of the artist in motion and make the life-sap rise
must be properly subjugated before they intoxicate us, and must
finally be made to submit to the law; Apollo demands it'. The

*The Fairy's Kiss: Margot
Fonteyn in Frederick Ashton's
version for the Vic-Wells
Ballet, London 1935*

'Apollonian' and 'Dionysian' in Picasso: *Four Dancers,* a drawing of 1925

Following page, the finale of Frederick Ashton's 1961 production of *Persephone* at the Royal Opera House, Covent Garden

recognition that 'Dionysian elements' are essential to the genesis of a work is significant.

It is a disconcerting experience to find distinct echoes of *Apollo* in Stravinsky's next ballet *The Fairy's Kiss,* since this, like *Pulcinella,* is a recomposition of music by another composer, in this case Tchaikovsky (exclusively songs and piano pieces – music that Tchaikovsky never orchestrated himself). It is certainly Apollonian in its graceful euphony, but here the references to the past are both more literal than usual (the Tchaikovsky citations are genuine) and more complex, since Stravinsky altered the originals with greater freedom than he had Pergolesi's in *Pulcinella* and, in numerous passages, incorporated phrases that sound very like Tchaikovsky but are really his own 'forgeries'. Even the ballet's plot indirectly alludes to Tchaikovsky's *The Sleeping Beauty* (a fairy 'marks' a young child with her magic kiss; years later she reappears on his wedding day, kisses him again and now claims him for ever), while in its curious absence

of motivation, its seeming inevitability, it also has links with the
'ritual' aspects of *Apollo*.

The limpid lyricism of *Apollo* and *The Fairy's Kiss* are recaptured
in *Persephone*, but here the subjugation of the Dionysian to the
Apollonian is placed, despite the classical source of the text, in a
specifically Christian and ritual context. The work was commissioned
by the wealthy actress and dancer Ida Rubinstein, who wanted a
central role that she could both speak and dance. She directed
Stravinsky to André Gide's poem, written over twenty years earlier,
in which Persephone is not abducted to the underworld, but descends
to Hades voluntarily out of compassion for those who dwell there.
The collaboration with Gide was not a happy one; the writer was so
offended by what he must have seen as Stravinsky's wilful distortions
of French prosody that he failed to appear at any of the rehearsals
or the performances. The work also is often seen as unhappy, with its

'When I first played the
music to him ... he would
only say "c'est curieux,
c'est très curieux", and
disappeared as soon
afterwards as possible':
Stravinsky with André Gide,
Wiesbaden 1933

awkward combination of speech and song, Gide's incoherent dramaturgy and a range of stylistic reference that is disconcertingly broad
even by Stravinsky's standards. These include, in the exquisite lullaby
over the sleeping Persephone, an apparent homage to Berlioz, a
composer Stravinsky had admired in his youth but later dismissed as
incompetent. His handling of the text here is particularly cavalier,
musical accents frequently falling on unaccented syllables, and it is
no surprise to learn that he drafted the chorus to a Russian text. He
sketched it 'from life', as a portrait of Vera Sudeikina asleep, but it is
not the only passage that achieves a sort of innocent radiance, giving
the work, along with *Apollo* itself, a central position among
Stravinsky's Apollonian scores.

    Persephone was followed by the Concerto for two solo pianos, and
by its orchestral counterpart in terms of 'abstract' neo-classicism –
in which, that is, allusions to the past are manipulated in thoroughly
Stravinskian ways, but with the references now almost vestigial –
the Concerto in E flat for chamber orchestra known as 'Dumbarton
Oaks'. (The name is that of the home near Washington of Mr and
Mrs Robert Woods Bliss, the American patrons who commissioned
it.) Stravinsky was happy enough to acknowledge Bach's
'Brandenburg' concertos as his point of departure, but the allusions
are glancing and sidelong; 'neo-Baroque' here is hard to distinguish
from 'neo-Symphonies of Wind Instruments' or 'neo-*Pribaoutki*'.

    Stravinsky's development in the years following *Mavra* and the
Octet is that of a man who has found a clear path forward, and is
methodically adding work to work in a carefully planned sequence.
A group of three pieces designed for himself to play (the Piano
Concerto, Sonata and the Serenade in A, all referring to classical
formal schemes), was followed by his very first religious work, a brief,
chant-like 'Pater noster' for unaccompanied chorus, originally written
to a syllabically set Slavonic text and intended for liturgical use.
Oedipus Rex, marking a new phase in his relationship with the past,
was followed by a further work for Stravinsky's concert repertoire
(the Capriccio) and two ballets on mythical or allegorical subjects
(*Apollo* and *The Fairy's Kiss*).

    The direction pointed by the 'Pater noster' and *Oedipus Rex* con-
tinued with the Symphony of Psalms; then the series of solo works
in classical forms was resumed (in the Violin Concerto and *Duo*

'Dumbarton Oaks',
Washington DC, the home
of Mr and Mrs Robert
Woods Bliss, who
commissioned Stravinsky's
Concerto in E flat to
celebrate their thirtieth
wedding anniversary.
The concerto was named
after the house and
given its first performance
there in 1938.

concertant). Another unaccompanied choral prayer in Slavonic, the Credo, preceded another sacred–secular ritual drama (*Persephone*), followed by another 'classical' solo keyboard work (the Concerto for two pianos), another quasi-ritual ballet (*Jeu de cartes* – the rituals here being those of the game of poker) and a final prayer-setting, the 'Ave Maria'.

Only with the approach of war did the orderly progression of works begin to stumble: a *Praeludium* for jazz band, probably intended as part of a suite, remained unpublished and unperformed for thirty years. The *Petit Ramusianum harmonique*, a sort of 'singing telegram' for the sixtieth birthday of Stravinsky's friend and colleague C. F. Ramuz, is a mere trifle. The Concerto in E flat ('Dumbarton Oaks') and the first two movements of a Symphony in C, commissioned by the Chicago Symphony Orchestra for its fiftieth anniversary, seem to suggest a thread being picked up, but two important musical and biographical facts are disguised by the self-assured progression of Stravinsky's works during the later years of his residence in France. First that *Persephone* – dating from twenty years after his exile from Russia – was his first extended setting of the French language; it was also his last. In the year of its completion he became

Stravinsky at Voreppe,
near Grenoble, with his
mother, 1932

a French citizen, and one year later sought election to the Institut de France. He was deeply humiliated by receiving only five of a possible thirty-two votes. Second, and in contrast, the Symphony of Psalms, the Violin Concerto, *Apollo*, *Jeu de cartes*, 'Dumbarton Oaks' and the Symphony in C were all written in response to commissions from the USA, which he had first visited for a highly successful and profitable concert tour in 1925, returning in 1935 and 1937.

5

Stravinsky in 1951

Can a composer re-use the past and at the same time move in a forward direction? Regardless of the answer (which is 'yes'), this academic question did not trouble me …

Stravinsky: *Themes and Episodes*

A Refugee in America 1939–51

It was not only the outbreak of war that made 1939 the end of a phase
in Stravinsky's life. His wife never recovered from the profound shock
of the death of their elder daughter from tuberculosis in the winter of
1938, and died herself the following spring, shortly followed by
Stravinsky's mother. Stravinsky was in poor health himself, spending
five months in the sanatorium where his wife and daughter had died.
Professionally his successful tours in America contrasted strongly with
his career in Europe, where several major works had recently been
coldly received. On one of the American tours he discovered that the
warm, clean air of California relieved the symptoms of his lung
condition. He had been offered and had accepted the Charles Eliot
Norton Professorship at Harvard University for the academic year
1939/40, which involved a course of six lectures and some informal
sessions with advanced students, but no regular teaching. The
Symphony in C, requested for the fiftieth anniversary of the Chicago
Symphony Orchestra, was half-finished. A friend described him at
this period as nervous, irritable, unable to work, eat or sleep, wanting
only to get out of Europe, 'into America, where life was still orderly'.

'Orderly' is the crucial word. Stravinsky was not, unlike many
other members of the expatriate community in America, a political
refugee from Nazism. He loathed the Nazis and filled scrapbooks
with press-cuttings about them embellished with his own derogatory
remarks, but he went out of his way to court and flatter Mussolini.
When the Nazi press described him as Jewish he did not ignore it; far
less, like Bartók, state publicly that he wished to be regarded as a Jew.
He hastily denied it; the greater part of his European income came
from Germany. Later, in America, he sympathized with composers
caught up in the anti-Communist 'witch-hunts' after the war, but was
reluctant to sign public declarations in their favour. His attitude to
politics is perhaps indicated in a reminiscence by the composer
Nicolas Nabokov. Shortly after the USA joined the war, Stravinsky
apparently became worried that some sort of revolution might be

Stravinsky in 1946, at a
rehearsal at the New York
City Centre of George
Balanchine's new
production of *The Fairy's
Kiss* for the Ballets Russes
de Monte Carlo

possible even in America. He asked an acquaintance whether this was
likely. Receiving the answer 'Maybe, maybe not', his immediate
reaction, 'in an appalled and indignant tone' was, 'But where will I
go?'. His only personal experience of political upheaval had been the
Russian Revolution, which had deprived him of financial security, of
his mother-tongue and of his nationality: he remained officially
stateless for twenty years. As with most of the events in his life he
preferred to talk only of the musical effects of this uprooting, but his
deepest political instinct was a fear of disorder.

On the outbreak of war he and Vera returned from the sanatorium
to her Paris flat, where air-raid alarms caused them to spend the night

Stravinsky and Vera,
newly naturalized American
citizens, 1940

In the garden at North Wetherly
Drive, 1941 (left to right): the
painter and stage designer
Eugene Berman, Stravinsky,
Vera, the photographer Baron
Gayne de Meyer

sheltering in the basement. Stravinsky fled to the country house of his admirer and disciple, the influential teacher Nadia Boulanger, whose composition pupils included almost every American composer of consequence to mature in the 1920s and 1930s, and who had many friends in the USA. Here he awaited the sailing of the ship in which, at the end of September 1939, he left France for New York. Officially, he was a French citizen visiting the USA on business, but on leaving Mlle Boulanger's he gave away his car, as though acknowledging that he would not be using it again. Vera, who as a Russian citizen needed a visa to enter the USA, joined him in January 1940. They were married in March and soon after applied for American citizenship.

Stravinsky's name was well-known in America, thanks to his concert tours and the advocacy of Koussevitzky and Nadia Boulanger (her classes in Paris and Fontainebleau were described by Cocteau as 'pas l'école de Stravinsky, mais l'église de Stravinsky'). As early as the First World War, long before his first visit to the USA, a newspaper report suggesting that he was sick and destitute in Switzerland had produced kindly donations of over $10,000. His removal to the USA, though, was a change not only of passport and climate. It was a change of economic climate also, and Stravinsky's first years in America were studded with unsuccessful attempts to cope with this. There were several projects to write film-scores, all of them abortive, music for some of them eventually recycled in various ways. He wrote a tango which the jazz musician Benny Goodman performed but never recorded; Stravinsky hoped that a popular song based on it and a version for dance-band might follow, but neither did. He accepted a commission to write a polka for a parade of circus elephants, wrote more music for jazz bands and contributed a short ballet score to a Broadway revue.

Domestically his adaptation to the New World proceeded smoothly. He stayed near Harvard for the period of his lectureship, lived in Boston briefly, but within six months moved to the Los Angeles area where he stayed until nearly the end of his life: North Wetherly Drive, West Hollywood was to be his home for twenty-eight years.

It was his and Vera's first home together. The house was neither large nor expensive. Though it cost less than $14,000, Stravinsky was obliged to take out a mortgage for about four-fifths of its price. It had only one bedroom; visitors were accommodated on a couch for which they were carefully measured (exceptionally tall guests needing an extra chair for their feet), their heights recorded and signed on the door frame. A single-storey building, it was set well back from the road in an ample garden which, during their earlier years there, the Stravinskys were obliged to dedicate to the war effort, giving over part of the ground to vegetables and, until neighbours protested, keeping chickens.

The house seems to have combined Vera's taste – modern furniture, many flowers, her own paintings as well as those received as gifts from friends such as Picasso, Chagall and Léger – and Stravinsky's passion for order. His study was sound-proof – his acute sensitivity to noise was combined with an inability to compose if he knew he was being overheard – and equipped with double, cork-lined doors. If the outer door was left open, Vera was allowed to enter, if both were closed not even she. Next to the upright piano at which he worked was what several visitors compared to a surgeon's instrument table, laid with meticulously arranged pens, including an implement that Stravinsky himself invented for drawing staves, pencils, erasers, knives, coloured inks, gums, stopwatches and

The dining room at North Wetherly Drive, 1945 (left to right): Stravinsky, Madeleine Milhaud, Darius Milhaud, Nadia Boulanger

metronomes. The piano itself was fitted up as a desk, with a sheet of plywood fixed to the music rack, large enough to accommodate the pages on which he was currently working plus sketches and other notes.

Another room was set aside as Vera's studio. In California she took up painting, exhibiting quite widely and frequently from the early 1950s. She became joint proprietor of a commercial art gallery, 'La Boutique', nearby on La Cienega Boulevard. Her studio was seldom visited by her husband, who claimed that strong smells affected his aural sense. For the same reason, his own workroom was placed as far from the kitchen as possible.

Stravinsky became as assiduous a book collector as his father, but in a far wider range of languages. Books on art were the largest group, with, according to Vera, poetry and detective stories vying for second place. Stravinsky owned, and constantly used, sufficient dictionaries for them to constitute a library in themselves. Ornaments, souvenirs and objects collected on their travels filled many shelves and small tables, and Stravinsky's archive of personal documents was so large that, when he and his wife eventually moved to a larger house in the same street, it filled several rooms. He also collected, especially in his later years but always to an obsessive degree, medicines.

Los Angeles attracted many refugee writers and artists during the late 1930s and 1940s. The great German novelist Thomas Mann described wartime Hollywood as 'a more intellectually stimulating and cosmopolitan city than Paris or Munich had ever been' and Vera Stravinsky enjoyed recalling that during their early years there Bertolt Brecht had produced a revised text of his *Galileo*, with music by Hanns Eisler, and Charles Laughton in the title-role, all three then being resident in Los Angeles. The Stravinskys' closest circle immediately after their arrival was made up mostly of Russians (understandably, since Stravinsky's English at that time was halting, Vera's almost non-existent): the choreographers George Balanchine and Adolph Bolm, the painter and stage designer Eugene Berman and the actor Vladimir Sokoloff (once a colleague of Vera's at the Kamerny Theatre in Moscow). Most of their other friends were ex-patriates, like Artur Rubinstein, Nadia Boulanger, the writer Franz Werfel and the violinist Joseph Szigeti, to all of whom Stravinsky generally spoke French or German.

Hollywood in the 1940s:
Sunset Boulevard at the
intersection with Vine Street.
Stravinsky lived about five
miles from this spot, on the
border of Hollywood and
Beverly Hills

Aldous Huxley, 1948. 'Of the learned people I know, he is the most delectable conversationalist.'

Vera's diary of the war years, however (Stravinsky himself seldom kept one, more often only a sketchy engagement book), indicates the intellectual climate of the city they had adopted and the rapidity with which they made themselves at home there. She records meetings, professional or social, with many musicians, whether resident in the city (Otto Klemperer, José Iturbi) or visitors to it (Sir Thomas Beecham, Heitor Villa-Lobos). The Stravinskys also circulated, no doubt partly because of hopes to secure contracts for film scores, among the aristocracy of Hollywood; Edward G. Robinson, Charlie Chaplin, John Houseman and Charles Laughton became quite close friends; René Clair, Mary Pickford, Bette Davis and even Greta Garbo were at least acquaintances. Max Reinhardt, Alma Mahler (by now married to Franz Werfel), Lion Feuchtwanger and Erich Maria Remarque were among their other hosts or guests. Vera, who made assiduous progress with her English, was for some time coached in it by another new friend, Anita Loos, the author of *Gentlemen Prefer Blondes*.

By the early 1950s many of Los Angeles' wartime expatriates had returned to Europe, and the pattern of the Stravinskys' friendships changed also. By now the names most frequently mentioned in Vera's diaries are those of Aldous Huxley and his wife Maria, closely followed by Christopher Isherwood, Gerald Heard and W. H. Auden. But Vera's diaries of the earlier 1940s, apart from recording the names of very many Russians among their closest associates (and for a long while the Stravinskys' servants were exclusively Russian), also mark regular visits to a Russian Orthodox church in Los Angeles, for communion on her husband's birthday (on Vera's birthday, 7 January, they would have received communion in any case, it being the Orthodox Christmas), and for Masses on the anniversaries of Catherine Stravinsky's death and that of her daughter.

Although Stravinsky eventually became idiomatically (if also idiosyncratically) fluent in English, with an impressively broad range of reading in it, Russian remained his 'first' language; that English ever truly became his second is unlikely. Five years after leaving France, switching on his radio for news of the war in Europe, he heard an announcement that Paris had been liberated and joyfully

W. H. Auden, from a detail of a drawing by Don Bachardy. 'I wonder whether any poet since the Elizabethans has made a composer such a beautiful gift of words ...'

wrote on the manuscript that he was working on, 'Paris n'est plus aux allemands!'. Stravinsky had spent much of World War I coming to terms with the loss of Russia and of Russian. It is hardly surprising that it took some time to come to terms with another war, another exile and another language. Whereas the sequence of works composed during his latter years in France suggests a composer methodically adding work to work, filling gaps in a pattern of which he is in firm control, the compositions of his first American decade suggest no such certainty of direction.

The would-be commercial Tango and the completion of the Symphony in C were his first tasks. The latter's style is 'new' only in the sense that Stravinsky had not written a purely instrumental symphony for over thirty years. But his change of continents is almost tangible as the lyrical slow movement gives way to an abrupt, nervous scherzo, while the subtitle of the lugubrious introduction to the finale might well be 'A Russian [feeling anything but at home] in New York'.

It was followed by a series of works in which commercial necessity – even opportunism – was a far more important impetus than any sense of stylistic direction. An elegant arrangement for small orchestra of the 'Bluebird' *pas de deux* from Tchaikovsky's *The Sleeping Beauty,* written for a ballet company many of whose players had joined the Army, was followed by a harmonization of 'The Star-Spangled Banner' that Stravinsky vainly hoped would become the 'authorized' version (and presumably profitable as a consequence). It was not widely used, and when Stravinsky planned to perform it in Boston he was informed by the police authorities that it infringed a state law against 'tampering with national property' and that, if he proceeded, the orchestral parts would be forcibly removed.

With *Danses concertantes*, a work commissioned for concert use, Stravinsky showed commercial acumen by casting it in the form of an abstract ballet, doubtless hoping that it would receive greater currency if a dance company were to take it into their repertoire. (One did: George Balanchine choreographed it two years later). It was followed by a commercial composition that was at least newsworthy: the *Circus Polka,* written for a parade of elephants at the Barnum and Bailey Circus. The elephants apparently found Stravinsky's rhythms awkward, but the piece had over four hundred performances. The

Four Norwegian Moods, however – coolly straightforward orchestral settings of folk melodies – were no more than an adroit salvaging of music drafted but rejected for a film about the Norwegian resistance. The *Ode* for orchestra, commissioned by Koussevitzky as one of a series of works in memory of his wife, has similar origins: the second of its three movements was originally written for a projected film score for *Jane Eyre*. Orson Welles, playing Mr Rochester, suggested the approach to Stravinsky, but the commission eventually went to Bernard Herrmann.

Babel, a brief cantata commissioned by the music publisher Nathaniel Shilkret as part of a planned collaborative work, a cycle of settings from the Book of Genesis by ten different composers, is perhaps the nadir of Stravinsky's commissioned work. In the event three of the most eminent composers who were approached (Bartók, Hindemith and Prokofiev) failed to take part and the work as finally performed has outer movements by Schoenberg (who was also finding it hard to adjust to the economic climate of America) and Stravinsky, separated by contributions from distinctly secondary figures: Shilkret himself, Alexandre Tansman, Darius Milhaud, Mario Castelnuovo-Tedesco and Ernst Toch; it was, though, Stravinsky's first setting of English words.

The *Scherzo à la russe* is another by-product of an abortive war film, this time set in Russia. On receiving a commission from the band-leader Paul Whiteman Stravinsky re-scored the piece for jazz band, but the music, a Russian dance close to that in *Petrushka*, has little to do with jazz and was subsequently arranged for symphony orchestra. *Scènes de ballet*, commissioned for a Broadway revue and owing something of its style to that fact, was later described by Stravinsky as 'a period piece, a portrait of Broadway in the last years of the War'; the score was heavily cut for its Broadway run.

The Sonata for two pianos, in some ways an appendix to the earlier Concerto for two solo pianos, suggests something of Stravinsky's state of mind at this time. It curiously looks both backwards, in its extensive use of Russian folk melodies, and forwards, in its fascination with strict canonic procedures. The first truly major work of Stravinsky's American years, the Symphony in Three Movements, did not arrive until the very end of World War II; he had been working on it fitfully over a period of more than three years.

Scènes de ballet: Margot Fonteyn, *opposite*, in Frederick Ashton's version choreographed for the Sadler's Wells Ballet, London 1948, with costume design by André Beaurepaire

Three images that
contributed to the genesis
of Stravinsky's Symphony
in Three Movements:
above, Nazi troops
parading before the
Brandenburg Gate in Berlin;
above right, a scene from
Henry King's 1943 film
The Song of Bernadette
(with Jennifer Jones, centre,
as Bernadette of Lourdes);
below right, a group of
Chinese peasants chipping
stones to lay a runway
for military aircraft

Of all his later works it is the one in which he came closest to acknowledging external sources as its 'inspiration': parts of the first movement were suggested by a documentary film about the effects of the war in China (Japanese 'scorched earth' tactics and shots of peasants working in the fields), the beginning of the finale by news-reel footage of goose-stepping German soldiers and its later pages by similar coverage of Allied successes. The central slow movement was originally composed for yet another film whose score was eventually entrusted to someone else (in this case to Alfred Newman), *The Song of Bernadette*, based on the book by Franz Werfel; the music was to have accompanied the Virgin Mary's miraculous apparition at Lourdes.

Other works of the immediate post-war years all in some ways revisit Stravinsky's past. The *Ebony Concerto* is again jazz-inspired, commissioned and first performed by the clarinettist Woody Herman and his band. The Concerto in D, a work in similar mould to 'Dumbarton Oaks', was Stravinsky's first European commission for a dozen years, requested by the wealthy Swiss conductor and patron Paul Sacher. Only by the late 1940s did Stravinsky take incisive steps forward with the last of his neo-classical ballet scores, *Orpheus*, and a long-gestated setting of the Mass.

Before finishing either of these latter works Stravinsky visited an exhibition of English art at the Chicago Art Institute, and was imme-diately impressed by the dramatic possibilities of Hogarth's *The Rake's Progress*. Their strong narrative (a young man is tempted by the pleasures of London, gives himself up to excess and ends in Bedlam) is reinforced by Hogarth's imagery, which often gives a strong impression of the scenes being played out on a stage. By this time Stravinsky's instinct for methodically ensuring that he wrote what he needed to write must have returned. Although he had wanted, he said, to write a dramatic work in English ever since arriving in America, he did not immediately announce this decision. He may have given something away by the interest he showed in the first American performances of *The Rape of Lucretia* by Benjamin Britten, a composer upon whom he was later to bestow few compliments, but of whose position as already the leading composer of opera in English he must have been aware.

Caricature of Stravinsky
by Walt Disney,
Hollywood 1939

Stravinsky's relationship to Britten is a curious one. He half-acknowledged that there was a relationship by admitting that his very last work, the Requiem Canticles, was to have been given the title *Sinfonia da Requiem*, but 'I did not use it only because I seem to have shared too many titles and subjects with Mr Britten already'. He had indeed: he chose a text already set by Britten (in his Serenade) to frame the canons of his Cantata, and included in *The Flood* a scene where the animals are called into the Ark to the same text that Britten chose for his *Noye's Fludde* (and the word-setting here is not dissimilar). Britten's Canticle *Abraham and Isaac* combines the two

protagonists' voices to personify the voice of God; Stravinsky, again in
The Flood, gives the words of God to two singers; his next work was
Abraham and Isaac. It seems hardly possible that these 'sharings' were
mere coincidences. Stravinsky's public comments about Britten and
his music were few and disdainful. He seems to have been fascinated
despite himself with what Britten was doing. This has been ascribed
to jealousy, but it is surely a complex jealousy: of a conspicuously
successful junior, of a junior moreover who largely managed to avoid
Stravinskian influence, and of a composer with whom he shared a
publisher, Boosey and Hawkes. He often asked to be sent copies
of Britten's scores (and found *Gloriana* at least 'very interesting'), but
when reporting the New York critics' 'abusive' response to his
own *Abraham and Isaac* in 1964 he added, 'And I really tried! Well,
what can you do, not everybody can have Benjamin Britten's success
with the critics.'

Not until *Orpheus* was complete and the Mass nearly so did he
tell his publisher that he was about to undertake, and with no
commission, by far his longest work to date, having estimated that it
would take until his seventieth year to complete. He also reported that
he had W. H. Auden in mind as his librettist (Auden's only previous
operatic collaboration, probably unknown to Stravinsky, was on
the operetta *Paul Bunyan*, written in 1941 for Benjamin Britten). Two
months later, after a preliminary meeting with Auden, he wrote again
to his publisher asking for scores of Mozart's *The Marriage of Figaro*,
Don Giovanni and *Così fan tutte*, Handel's *Messiah* and *Israel in
Egypt* and the Glyndebourne recordings of the three Mozart operas.

Stravinsky's works of the 1940s therefore make a puzzling progression. War and renewed financial insecurity undoubtedly disrupted
his sense of direction and led to time-consuming work in areas that
proved to be dead ends. For the *Jane Eyre* film project, for example,
Stravinsky sketched not only the single scene that was re-used in the
Ode but several others, and went to great trouble to improve his
English sufficiently to read Charlotte Brontë's novel and Mrs Gaskell's
biography of her in the original. Much time was also spent, especially
in the immediately post-war years when Stravinsky had acquired a
new publisher, in revising his earlier works. His aim was partly to
make the fuller-scored pieces accessible to smaller orchestras, partly to
incorporate genuine second thoughts and improvements (the revised

Benjamin Britten (c. 1947),
whose admiration for
Stravinsky was not reciproc-
ated (the older composer
referred to the younger as
'Aunt Britten' and scoffed at
the 'Battle-of-Britten
sentimentality' surrounding
his War Requiem)

1947 score of *Petrushka* reveals the older Stravinsky severely correcting the 'extravagances' of his younger self). Most imperatively he needed to safeguard his copyright position. For many years neither the USA nor the Soviet Union were signatories to the Berne Convention, and Stravinsky's popular early ballets were widely played in their original versions without earning him any income. During his American years his earnings as a performer always exceeded those from composition. The immensely time-consuming work of tran-scribing his earlier music – *The Firebird* took longer to revise than to compose – was an attempt, largely unsuccessful, to alter this balance.

Amid all these distractions, digression became a theme of Stravinsky's early years in America; not since the time of *Les Noces* were so many works interrupted, put aside or delayed. His long-meditated setting of the Mass, begun in 1944, had to wait four years before he could complete it; the Symphony in Three Movements took three years to finish. It would be going too far to suggest that Stravinsky sensed the onset of his second 'creative crisis', but amid the diversions a gradual sense of forward progress did eventually reassert itself and, in retrospect, his neo-classical years ended with a very satisfying sense of culmination.

The four ballet scores of this period – *Jeu de cartes* was written in France but for an American company and clearly belongs with its successors, *Danses concertantes, Scènes de ballet* and *Orpheus* – can seem like a series of false starts and a curiously delayed arrival. The first three are relatively light in weight, and have been dismissed as 'minor' Stravinsky without taking account of the humour and game-playing that was an intermittent but constant factor in his music. Some of his earliest, now lost compositions were comic songs and musical jokes, his very last a setting of Edward Lear's *The Owl and the Pussy-Cat*. Alongside its rhythmic heft and at times elegantly spare lines, *Jeu de cartes* is fundamentally good-humoured, even brash, with clever quotations and half-quotations from Tchaikovsky, Beethoven, Ravel, Johann Strauss and Rossini. *Danses concertantes* is a continuation of this vein, as well as of Stravinsky's line of abstract, 'white' ballets, all the more so since it was originally written for concert performance. *Scènes de ballet*, composed for a commercial revue, is a shrewd response to such a commission, 'compromising' with Broadway to the extent of including a trumpet tune that refers to Broadway originals to no greater and no lesser extent than previous Stravinsky scores had 'referred' to Bach, Glinka or Verdi.

With *Orpheus* Stravinsky returned to the line of *Apollo* and *Persephone*, even of *Oedipus Rex*, but in a distilled form demonstrating that his Apollonian manner was capable of further development. It is austere both in its scoring, so reticent that its orchestra sounds smaller than it is, and in its quietness: only once does the music rise above *forte*. Expressively it is perhaps the ultimate Stravinskian paradox. Essaying no bold gestures or even raising its voice it is nevertheless both poignantly moving (in the *pas de deux* for the re-united Orpheus and Eurydice) and terrifyingly violent (the *pas d'action* in which the Bacchantes seize Orpheus and tear him to pieces; the ballet's only *fortissimo* occurs briefly at the climax of this otherwise sinisterly hushed music). References to the past are there, the beautiful *pas de deux* echoing Tchaikovsky's Serenade for Strings, Orpheus's *air de danse* being another of Stravinsky's neo-Baroque arias. Yet there is a further paradox: few of Stravinsky's later scores sound so suavely melodious, though long melodic lines are few. Hints at the post-neo-classical future are also to be found: a preoccupation with precisely scored and spaced chords as sonic objects, an angularity of melodic outline, a liking for severe counterpoint.

The two symphonies, composed at the war's beginning and its end, are oddly contrasted. The Symphony in C is a distinctly balletic work, a transitional symphony not only in its sudden memory of Russia in the dark prelude to the finale. The scherzo, the first move-ment to be written in America, has an almost hectic brilliance that may reflect Stravinsky's awareness of his new continent, especially as the opening idea is immediately followed by another of pronouncedly Russian cast. The frenetic optimism of the finale concludes with a sequence of slow, quiet chords that looks back to the ritually solemn endings of several of his Russian works, and at the same time forward to the austere religious works of his late years.

The Symphony in Three Movements shares this Janus-like character (the syncopated rhythms in its outer movements are very close to *The Rite of Spring*, while on other pages the music looks clearly into the future). Its contrapuntal devices are developed in part from the Symphony of Psalms but their bony angularity anticipates aspects of Stravinsky's late style. It is hard to say whether the agitated

Orpheus: Isamu Noguchi's
costume designs for the
first production (1948)
with choreography by
George Balanchine

Orpheus: Nicholas
Magallanes in the title
role, with Tanaquil Le
Clercq as the Leader of
the Bacchantes, New
York 1948

beginning of the coda to the finale (for harp and low strings, a 'late
Stravinsky' sound) is closer to the *pas d'action* for the Bacchantes in
Orpheus or to the double *pas de quatre* in his proto-serial ballet *Agon*
of 1957. And yet the Symphony is, in its frequent use of obstinately
repeated short melodic fragments constructed from few notes,
another of Stravinsky's 'Russian' works. As the source of its slow
movement in an unrealized film score indicates, it is also a collection
of disparate material that eventually and protractedly became a
symphony rather than a work planned with Stravinsky's customary
meticulousness. The first movement, drafted in 1942, has an important piano part, and one of Stravinsky's friends understood the
work was then intended as a piano concerto. The slow movement,
perhaps because of its association with the vision at Lourdes, features
the harp no less prominently. The finale, as though to 'resolve' this

'A toast, ladies and
gentlemen: to Venus and to
Mars!': the Tavern Scene
from Hogarth's *A Rake's
Progress* (1735), corres-
ponding to Act I, scene 2
('Mother Goose's Brothel')
of Stravinsky's opera

problem, gives both instruments a leading role, especially in a quasi-fugal section that is one of the work's most prophetic passages.

The 'occasional' works of these years also seem indecisively poised between past and future. *Babel* begins with a recollection of *The Firebird*'s opening pages and with vaguely Russian lyricism, but at the horus's first entry the language of the Symphony of Psalms and Symphonies of Wind Instruments is clearly striving to develop further. Passages of the coolly lyrical *Ode* sound like sketches for the matured 'late neo-classicism' of *Orpheus*; the very opening is startlingly similar to much later music in which Stravinsky articulated his personal response to serialism. Even the *Ebony Concerto*, the most extended of his jazz essays, is at least as fascinated with the unaccustomed sonorities of Woody Herman's band as it is with the rhythmic and melodic hallmarks of jazz. The work is, like 'Dumbarton Oaks' and the Concerto in D, a sort of *concerto grosso* or 'Brandenburg' concerto, scored for solo clarinet with six saxophones (two altos, two tenors, baritone and bass), horn, five trumpets, three trombones, piano, harp (!), guitar, double bass and percussion. Stravinsky absorbedly puts this darkly shining ensemble to quite un-jazz-like uses.

The work of this period that most strongly suggests a composer at last sensing a new forward path is the Mass which Stravinsky completed – without a commission or much likelihood that it would be performed, as he hoped, liturgically – in 1948. In an attempt to write a 'real' Mass (provoked into doing so, he said, by the 'rococo-operatic sweets of sin' that he found in Mozart's masses) he adapted to his own style many techniques characteristic of the ancient musical language of the Church: linear and chordal chant, strict counterpoint, formalized ornament, strong contrast between solo and choral voices. It is a consciously archaizing work, in short, and this quality is emphasized by the bare scoring: the 'orchestra' consists of two each of oboes, cors anglais, bassoons, trumpets and trombones; the high voices, both solo and choral, should be boy trebles and altos. There are as many recollections of Stravinsky's past as in his other music of these years (hieratic choral textures rooted in the Symphony of Psalms, motor rhythms, melodies in his 'Russian' manner, repetitive and of narrow range) but the antique solemnity of the piece and its gaunt austerity announce a new phase.

David Hockney's set design
for the final scene, in
Bedlam, of *The Rake's
Progress* for the Glynde-
bourne production, 1975

The Mass was immediately followed by *The Rake's Progress*. It is interesting that directly after a corrective to Mozart's 'sweets of sin' Stravinsky should have turned to a conspicuously Mozartian opera. He was a good deal abused for this, accused of mere pastiche. In fact the choice of Mozart as such a riskily close model (Stravinsky's letter to his publisher requesting scores and recordings of Mozart's operas referred to them as 'the source of inspiration' for the as yet unwritten opera) was particularly astute, and the decision to write such an opera at all a courageous one.

It was his first major composition to an English text, and in plot it retreated radically from the mythical, ritual dramas that had been his preoccupation for thirty years. He had not attempted comedy before, with the exception of *Mavra* (very brief, and in his native language). It was also his first true opera, a form which he had distrusted ever since *The Nightingale*. The obvious model suggested by Hogarth's scenes is a light-weight ballad opera, but by announcing that Mozart was to be his inspiration it is obvious that Stravinsky wanted to clothe Hogarth's extremely basic plot with characterization and extra incident, with irony or ambiguity, with suggestions of mythic prototypes. Not *The Beggar's Opera* as model, in short, but *Don Giovanni* and *Così fan tutte*. He needed Mozart as a point of reference, and he needed a librettist of genius and musicality.

It was Aldous Huxley who put forward Auden's name, and Stravinsky described the fruit of this inspired suggestion as 'the most beautiful opera libretto since [Mozart's collaborator] da Ponte'. Auden's fluency – asked for additional verses in an awkward metre he complied by return of post – was only part of this. His knowledge and love of opera, of Mozartian opera especially, was crucial to the success of the partnership; so was a clear parallel between his ability to express an entirely modern sensibility within regular, even 'traditional' metres and rhyme-schemes and Stravinsky's own use of stylistic reference. Because composer and librettist were together at Stravinsky's home to draft the outline of the opera's plot and its division into numbers, and because Auden (and his co-author Chester Kallman) delivered the libretto with such efficient speed, little correspondence between the two exists. We are therefore unable to say whether the parallel between the opening scene of innocence in spring and the closing images of an imagined spring are due to

'What voice is this? What heavenly strains bring solace to tormented brains?': Hogarth's final scene of the Rake in Bedlam, dying in the arms of the girl he has abandoned, closely corresponds to Act III, scene 3 of Stravinsky's opera.

Auden or to Stravinsky. But the theme of cyclic renewal, from *The Rite of Spring* to *Persephone*, is as archetypally Stravinskian as its cunning artifice is Audenesque.

The opera's première, at the Teatro la Fenice in Venice on 11 September 1951, was an event of international significance, broadcast and discussed world-wide. It was followed by productions in many other cities, and *The Rake* has since come as close as any post-war opera to joining the standard repertoire. Yet its critical reception for many years was not effusive. In no score of Stravinsky's are the allusions to earlier styles, above all to Mozart, so transparently obvious. Those who had always resisted neo-classicism found *The Rake's Progress* brittle, facetious and barren. Stravinsky was particularly wounded by the opera's reception in Paris, where it was regarded as an irrelevant anachronism by those young musicians and composers who since the war had enthusiastically discovered Schoenberg and his school. His rejection by the young in the city where he had once been their undisputed leader was undoubtedly an important factor in prompting Stravinsky to forge a new and radical language as he entered his eighth decade.

Some perceived – though it took a long while for the perception to become general – that *The Rake's Progress* is archetypal Stravinsky from beginning to end, that while referring more closely to a model than ever before, he had managed triumphantly to remain himself.

Above, Stravinsky in Paris, 1953, for the first French production of *The Rake's Progress*, with his son Theodore and Jean Cocteau.

Opposite, Stravinsky rehearsing for the first production of *The Rake's Progress*

Very few can have guessed that his next step would be to retreat from neo-classicism, as always retaining his personal identity while embracing the techniques of the composer who had always been regarded as his antipole if not his rival, Arnold Schoenberg.

6

Stravinsky, c. 1958

*Of course, it requires greater effort to learn
from one's juniors, and their manners are not
invariably good. But when you are seventy-five
and your generation has overlapped with four
younger ones, it behoves you not to decide in
advance 'how far composers can go', but to try
to discover whatever new thing it is makes the
new generation new.*

Stravinsky: *Conversations with Igor Stravinsky*

The Second Crisis 1952–7

In February 1944 Stravinsky received a letter from Robert Craft, a twenty-year-old music student in New York, with various questions about his music and a request to borrow scores of works that had become difficult to obtain. Craft was already making a name for himself as a conductor of 'difficult' contemporary music and as a very capable promoter of his own concerts, often with ensembles of former fellow-students. Three years later the correspondence was resumed, and Stravinsky willingly replied to his questions and began to ask for the young man's help: to enquire why a recording was not available, to send scores to his pianist son Soulima, and so on. Craft has not published the majority of his own letters to the composer, but the older man was obviously impressed by his intelligence, understanding and musicality. He began to use him as a trustworthy intermediary in his dealings with publishers and others, and gladly collaborated in Craft's concert-giving activities, providing him with advice and

Stravinsky at a recording
session, assisted by
Robert Craft

information and even conducting certain works himself without a
fee. They first met in 1948, and in the following year Stravinsky
invited Craft to become his musical assistant. His first tasks were to
catalogue a collection of manuscripts and sketches that had been
left in France before the war and had now arrived in his Hollywood
home, and to advise on the stresses, pronunciation and precise
meanings of English words during the composition of *The
Rake's Progress*.

Craft was active in performing a wide range of twentieth-century
music, including that of Schoenberg and his school. In Los Angeles
he quite naturally took the opportunity to consult Schoenberg,
who lived nearby. Stravinsky maintained, at least in public, a reserved
attitude towards his great contemporary. Though the two lived no
more than ten miles apart, there was no contact between them. In an
interview as late as 1952 Stravinsky insisted that although the serial-
ists were the only composers with a discipline that he respected,
they were 'prisoners of the figure twelve, while I feel greater freedom
with the figure seven' (i.e., the seven notes of the major or minor
scale, as opposed to the twelve of the chromatic). With an avowed
Schoenbergian about the house, and hearing the music of Schoenberg
and his followers at Craft's concerts he embarked on a reappraisal of
what had been regarded as a technique and a style quite antithetical
to his own. After Schoenberg's death in 1951, Stravinsky began
very gradually and at first rather conservatively to adopt elements of
Schoenbergian technique, though it was to be several years before
he wrote a truly twelve-note serial work.

Schoenberg had invented this technique as a solution to a
perceived crisis: that 'advanced' music – late Wagner, Richard Strauss,
Schoenberg's own early works – had become so chromatic, using
so many notes extraneous to the supposedly prevailing key, that the
sense of key itself, the very basis of classical musical grammar and
form, was in danger of dissolution. Instinctively believing that
the forward progress of the art could not be stopped, Schoenberg
proposed a radical solution: that the inevitable be accepted, that the
days of tonality, of the functional use of the key system were over,
and that a new ordering principle to govern the micro- and the
macro-structure of music be adopted. It was, paradoxically, a conservative solution as well, since the 'crisis' was one affecting the Austro-

Stravinsky and Craft
at rehearsal

Right, Stravinsky in 1959,
with a copy of the first
Craft/Stravinsky
book *Conversations
with Igor Stravinsky*

Crayon portrait of
Stravinsky by Alberto
Giacometti, Paris,
October 1957

German tradition of which Schoenberg was a descendant, and
the function of the proposed solution was to save that tradition, in
however fundamentally altered a form.

Stravinsky's 'capitulation' to a style that was already becoming a
rigid orthodoxy in some quarters dismayed and repelled many of his
admirers. His one-time friend Ernest Ansermet, acknowledged by
Stravinsky as one of his finest interpreters, published a book intended
to refute serialism and all its advocates. Meeting Stravinsky again he
asked whether, if the producer of a play took one of its crucial lines,
reversed the order of its syllables and ended with a concerted shout of
all those syllables simultaneously, anyone would understand what
it meant. Stravinsky's reply was, 'Not necessarily, but the effect might
be interesting.'

As a Russian, from a musical culture that had already devised its
own alternatives to Austro-German symphonic form, Stravinsky
did not share Schoenberg's imperatives. He was not an heir to the
imperilled tradition that Schoenberg had tried to save. His music
had always stood at a tangent to traditional grammar and formal
structures, and having seldom used the sense of key for the purposes
that Wagner, Strauss and Schoenberg had weakened, he had no need
of a substitute for it.

Stravinsky was much more attracted by the fact that Schoenberg's
system was rigorously economical. By its use an entire composition
could be derived, by strictly observed permutational methods, from a
single cell of twelve notes, a 'row' constructed from all twelve notes of
the chromatic scale. In a sense Stravinsky had always been a 'serialist':
exhaustive investigation of the possibilities of a small group of notes
had been an important part of his composing process since his early
years. In *The Rite of Spring*, for example, the 'Spring Rounds' are built
from a 'row' of no more than four notes, and this is quite typical of
the score as a whole. By the early 1950s this had become an almost
instinctive process, rooted in the flexible melodies of narrow compass
that Stravinsky had found in Russian folk music and distilled into his
own style. But the process, though related to Schoenberg's practice,
was very far from his spirit. For Schoenberg it was essential – since his
method began from an acceptance of the decay of tonality – that
music using his system should never 'lapse' into a sense of key. Hence
his insistence that once any note had been sounded it should not be

used again until all eleven other notes of the chromatic scale had
been heard. Any repetition of a note would hint at that note's possible
primacy, an eventuality that the method was expressly designed to
avoid. Stravinsky's early 'serial' works deny this principle by freely
allowing repetition and by allowing, even encouraging, a sense of
key by building 'tone-rows' from far fewer notes than the canonical
twelve. Stravinsky, early in his 'conversion' to serialism, was more
interested in the intensification of his own inherent compositional
rigour than in any of the motives that had driven Schoenberg.

It was said of course that Stravinsky's serialism was a result of
Craft's proselytizing. Craft first denied this then asserted it, but the
phraseology of his denial ('as if anyone could even lead *that* horse to
water, if it didn't want to go, let alone make it drink') is revealing. All
that we know of Stravinsky's musical personality confirms that no
one could make him do anything. Yet there seems little doubt that in
the wake of *The Rake's Progress* he was in need of a rejuvenating
change of direction, a change predicted by the severe and archaizing
Mass. Neither Craft nor anyone else could have led him to serialism
if he had maintained his wilful refusal to notice it. Craft reported
that his ignorance at this time of the major works of Schoenberg and
his disciples Alban Berg and Anton Webern was almost total. But
since the horse did want to investigate the palatability of that water,
no one was better able than Craft perhaps not to 'lead' him to it but
to encourage him to examine it. Indeed without the presence of the
formidably well-informed Craft, it is doubtful whether Stravinsky
could have brought himself to study the works of those composers
whose names were used to belittle his own.

The first step was the Cantata that he began immediately after
The Rake's Progress. On his return to Hollywood he went to a concert
conducted by Craft that included Webern's Quartet Op. 22 and
Schoenberg's Suite Op. 29. He attended all the rehearsals and thus
heard both works several times. A few days later Stravinsky startled
both Craft and Mrs Stravinsky by breaking down in tears, saying that
he could no longer compose and did not know what to do. He was
persuaded, apparently, that this mood would pass, but it is hard not
to hear the central movement of the Cantata as a quite extraordinarily
creative, and brave, reaction to this crisis.

It takes the form of a setting of 'Tomorrow shall be my dancing day', that strange anonymous medieval allegory of Christ's passion, as a series of canons in which the theme is subjected to all the basic processes of serial technique. It is heard in inversion, retrograde and retrograde inversion (played, that is, backwards, upside-down and both backwards and upside-down). The theme is eleven notes long but, in a manner characteristic of Stravinsky for nearly forty years, it is built from only six close-set pitches, and has a strong sense of key. It thus has some of the rigour of genuine serial music while preserving Stravinsky's identity intact. A lesser composer would no doubt have gone further.

The Cantata does not *sound* like a serial work. Its cool and gracious lines and archaic flavour have close affinities with the Mass, and the use of strict canonic devices is not new in Stravinsky's work. But his realization that serial practice was not incompatible with his own language, that it offered that language opportunities to develop further, is clearly audible in the strangely gripping solemnity of the central movement. At Easter 1952, just over a month after his crisis of confidence, Stravinsky was able to present Craft with a manuscript leaf from the Cantata, a setting of the words 'And through the glass window shines the sun', inscribed 'To Bob whom I love'.

The Cantata was followed by, indeed overlapped with, a Septet in which Stravinsky expanded the newly discovered processes. Much of the piece still sounds close to his works of the preceding two decades, but a new exhilaration is audible in the way that he progressively discovers methods of deriving a whole contrapuntal texture from the ingenious manipulation of a 'row', now of eight pitches. The discovery reaches its climax in the brilliant final Gigue – its subtitle an overt homage to the last movement of Schoenberg's Suite – which is a double fugue, or rather a pair of double fugues, in which Stravinsky, with obvious and infectious pleasure, contrives that all his melodic lines shall be transposed variants of his eight-note cell.

One of his objectives in composing the Cantata was to investigate further the problems of setting English words. Auden offered him another libretto, the dramatic masque 'Delia', but Stravinsky did not respond; to accept it would possibly have implied some sort of 'sequel' to *The Rake's Progress*, and he was now moving in a radically different direction. A suggestion that he might collaborate with the

Following page, Stravinsky rehearsing with the BBC Symphony Orchestra, London, December 1958; his fee for a single concert was £900, three times as much as any other conductor engaged by the BBC at that time.

Welsh poet Dylan Thomas interested him, however, and the two met to discuss possible ideas. Thomas's proposal, a plot concerning the rediscovery of the Earth, including the rediscovery of language, after a nuclear disaster, excited Stravinsky sufficiently for him to invite the poet to Hollywood to develop the idea, and even to build a guest-room extension of the North Wetherly Drive house to receive him. Waiting for a telegram to announce the time of Thomas's arrival in Los Angeles, Stravinsky received only a request from the press for a comment on his sudden death the previous day in New York. He wept, and retreated into his study. A couple of months later he wrote a setting for tenor and string quartet of Thomas's elegy for his own father's death, 'Do not go gentle into that good night'. Only when he knew what other instrumentalists would be playing in the concert at which its first performance was scheduled did he add two 'dirge canons' as prelude and postlude, in which the string quartet is heard in grave dialogue with four trombones.

In memoriam Dylan Thomas was a more radical expansion of his serial practice. Its row or 'set' is of only five notes, within a characteristically Stravinskian narrow compass, but whereas the eight-note set of the Septet was a melody subjected to serial processes, that of *In memoriam Dylan Thomas* is a set from which the movingly expressive vocal line and every other element of the whole composition are derived.

All three of these works, Cantata, Septet and *In memoriam Dylan Thomas*, plus the sparely elegant Three Songs from William Shakespeare and even the diminutive *Greeting Prelude* (a 45-second subjection of 'Happy Birthday to You' to a jovial battery of serial devices, written for the eightieth birthday of his old friend the conductor Pierre Monteux) can be seen in retrospect as preparations for the three large-scale masterpieces to which Stravinsky devoted the years 1955–8.

Of these the ballet *Agon* (the Greek title means 'contest') had been on Stravinsky's desk since the end of 1953. George Balanchine and Lincoln Kirstein of the New York City Ballet had been begging him for another ballet score since shortly after *Orpheus* in 1948. They hoped that it might be on a classical subject, to complete a 'Greek trilogy' with *Apollo* and *Orpheus*.

'As soon as I saw him I
knew that the only thing to
do was to love him':
Dylan Thomas,
photographed in 1946

Left, Allegra Kent and Arthur
Mitchell in *Agon*, a revival
of George Balanchine's
1957 ballet for the
1972 Stravinsky Festival
in New York
Right and following page,
Stravinsky and Balanchine
during rehearsals for *Agon*
in 1957

Instead *Agon* is the last and perhaps the greatest of Stravinsky's 'white' abstract ballets, a work of exhilarating vividness, rhythmic élan and dazzling instrumental virtuosity. His first idea was for a suite of dances based on a seventeenth-century French dance manual, but his growing interest in Schoenbergian process influenced the work's conspicuous patterning in twelves: *Agon* has twelve scenes, the score is subtitled 'ballet for twelve dancers' and several of its movements are in multiples of twelve bars. This exactitude, and the refraction of the past implied by the references to archaic dance forms, are both paralleled in the uncanny precision of Stravinsky's instrumental imagination in this work. The extraordinary 'Gailliarde' (his mis-spelling) is perhaps the most striking example of this: a dignified, archaic processional is sounded by three cellos and viola, all very low in their compass and – octaves above – by three flutes and the almost flute-like sound of two double basses playing in harmonics; in the gulf between, mandolin and harp dance gravely in canon. We seem to be hearing a consort of lutes, viols and recorders, but from a great distance. Similar evocations of a past more remote than Stravinsky's normal frame of reference are heard in the neo-Renaissance fanfares of the opening *pas de quatre* and final quadruple trio (in the purest C major), while elsewhere the angularity and the bracingly wide-open spaces between instruments so characteristic of Webern are more than hinted at: the coda that succeeds the antique galliard marks Stravinsky's first use of a genuine (though still far from strictly used) twelve-note row. His relief, at the age of nearly seventy-five, at finding a rejuvenating new path seems to be another reason for *Agon*'s joyous ebullience.

7

Stravinsky at the BBC's
Maida Vale studios,
October 1961; a return visit
to conduct his *Persephone*

Le lyrisme n'existe pas sans règles ...

C.-A. Cingria: *Pétrarque*,
underlined by Stravinsky in his copy of the
book, presented to him by the author

Late Stravinsky 1958–71

Agon was begun in December 1953 but not completed until April
1957. He interrupted it to pay his homage to Dylan Thomas, then to
respond to a commission from Venice which, after St Petersburg,
was probably the city closest to his heart. He planned the *Canticum
sacrum* as a homage to the city's patron, St Mark, designed it specifically for performance in that saint's basilica (with carefully placed
pauses in the more fully-scored music to allow for the decay of
reverberation), and even reflected the five-domed plan of St Mark's
in his symmetrical five-movement structure. His next work, *Threni*,
commissioned by North German Radio, is still under the spell of
Venice (it was begun and given its first performance there) and
demonstrates a resurgence of Stravinsky's lifelong preoccupation with
ritual. At the same time, like the *Canticum sacrum*, it strongly suggests
that he had found in the rigour of serialism an ideal language for his
personal vision of the music of religious ritual.

The *Canticum sacrum* is not wholly serial, though its central
section very largely is. Curiously enough the most conspicuous example of serial practice is seen in the fact that the least 'advanced'
opening movement (vigorous brass writing and quiet organ interludes
paying direct homage to Venetian music) is subjected to strict retro-
gression: it is played backwards to form the finale. Between these, two
florid solo 'motets' almost in Monteverdi's manner enclose a tripartite
central movement (a eulogy of the three Christian virtues of charity,
faith and hope – in that order, faith at the centre) of grave canons and
austere instrumental processionals. It was found perplexing at first
hearing, and has never become a popular work. Some indication of
the reason for this is given by Stravinsky's own recording, in which a
very small choir and a scratch orchestra negotiate the notes by the
skin of their teeth in a pitilessly dry studio. Of the work's sheer beauty
of sound, of the spare eloquence of its long lines, of its deeply moving
pious intensity there is as little evidence as there is of any attempt
to provide the impressively reverberant acoustic for which it was so

Urbi Venetiae, in laude Sancti sui Presidis, Beati Marci Apostoli (dedication of the *Canticum sacrum*): Stravinsky, in Venice for the première, 1956

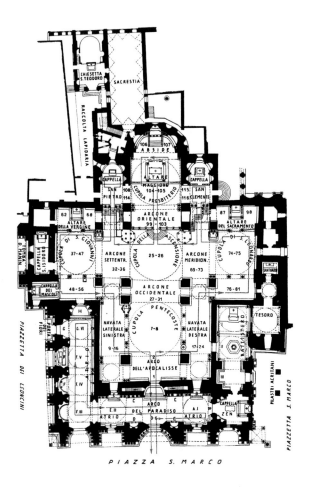

PIAZZA S. MARCO

The ground-plan of St
Mark's in Venice, its
symmetrical structure, five
domes approached through
an atrium, reflected in the
layout of Stravinsky's
Canticum sacrum

carefully designed. Stravinsky's late works, more than most music of
this century, are perilously misrepresented by merely adequate
performances.

Threni is wholly serial from beginning to end; indeed it is 'super-
serial' in the sense that Stravinsky goes well beyond a strict adoption
of Schoenbergian principle. In the works using rows of fewer than
twelve notes the lack of strictness could still have been seen as a compromise. In *Threni* the back-tracking repetitions within rows and
the mathematical games played with them are by no means ploys to
retain a toe-hold on tonality. They seem, rather, to be attempts at
finding a purely serial replacement for elements that had been

hallmarks of Stravinsky's earlier style (ostinato repetitions, for example, or the rigorous explorations of narrow-band 'sets') but which could no longer be maintained once the full fascination of serial rigour had taken hold. It is significant that this 'rotational' technique, as it came to be called, should first have been sketched in a sacred work, where the lines and textures to which it gives rise have an incantatory, ritual quality. In sacred music, too, there is an ancient and honourable tradition of arcane devices, unperceived by the profane listener, being used for the glory of God and the pleasure and pride of the craftsman.

With Stravinsky's return to secular composition, in the diamantine *Movements* for piano and orchestra of 1959, the full extent of his most abrupt change of direction became shockingly apparent. The rotational technique sketched in *Threni* is here elaborated into the most complex 'game' that he had ever played, a system of methodically 'shunting' intervals from the series like beads on an abacus. Why a particular note occupies a particular position can almost invariably be explained by reference to some aspect of strict serial practice, but why that aspect, that rationale was chosen rather than another is harder to determine. It is as though at the moment at which he most closely embraced strict serialism Stravinsky was eager to broaden the number of choices available to him at any given

Stravinsky at a BBC Symphony Orchestra rehearsal in London, October 1961; in his eightieth year, he now used a walking stick and was assisted at rehearsals by Robert Craft but had already that year given concerts or made recordings in New York, Toronto, Mexico, Finland, Sweden, Germany, Yugoslavia and Switzerland

Acknowledging applause in
Belgrade after conducting a
performance of *Persephone*,
September 1961

The return to Russia: after a concert in the Grand Hall of the Moscow Conservatoire in October 1962, Stravinsky is applauded by Tikhon Khrennikov, Secretary of the Union of Soviet Composers since the Zhdanov purges of 1948. At a public rehearsal Stravinsky had caused general but embarrassed laughter by assuring him that 'Even you, Tikhon Nikolayich, will be using serialism soon!'.

point, to avoid the series dictating to him and to keep his options continually open. Described in this way, the work sounds hermetic, more suited to analysis than to performance or to listening. And yet the explosive energy of the music and its extreme lucidity of texture make it an invigorating and enthralling experience in the concert-hall or on records. The precision of Stravinsky's ear is as evident as ever; the difficulty of the work lies in the extreme velocity with which its events arrive at the ear.

This difficulty is something of a constant in 'late Stravinsky', a phase that can be conveniently defined as beginning with *Movements*. Yet the piece is almost its most extreme case; all subsequent works (with the exception of the orchestral Variations in memory of Aldous Huxley), though they continue and elaborate the intransigent techniques of *Movements*, ameliorate its sheer density of event in one way or another. Some achieve this, since several of the late pieces are on sacred subjects, by recapturing the hieratic manner of *Canticum sacrum* and *Threni*. Seven of the eleven remaining works have texts, and of these two have elements of drama – in one even of comedy – that dictate an easier pace. Yet even here there are signs that the old Stravinsky's mind (he was seventy-seven when he finished *Movements*, eighty-four at the time of his last completed composition) moved with an astonishingly youthful, impatient vigour.

The creativity of the last years is indeed amazing. He suffered his first stroke as early as 1956 and was in poor health and under more or less constant medical attention for most of the remaining fifteen years of his life. He nevertheless continued to travel widely and to conduct many concerts and recordings until two years before his death. In 1962 for example, the year of his eightieth birthday, he gave concerts in Los Angeles, Washington, Seattle, Toronto, New York, Johannesburg, Springs (a Bantu township near Pretoria), Hamburg (for an eightieth birthday festival of his works), Chicago, Tel Aviv, Haifa, Jerusalem, Hollywood, Rome, Perugia and Caracas, as well as a four-week visit to Russia, his first for nearly half a century.

For many years his music had been rarely heard in the Soviet Union, his recent music not at all. Tikhon Khrennikov, First Secretary of the Composers' Union, had described Stravinsky as 'the apostle of reactionary forces in bourgeois music'. Dmitry Shostakovich, unquestionably the most important composer in

Opposite, June 1966: lunching at Le Grand Vefour in Paris, with Henri Cartier-Bresson, who took the photograph

Russia, had as recently as 1960 (albeit in a statement that he may have been compelled to make, since 'the unwholesome influence of Igor Stravinsky' had been detected in his own music) denounced Stravinsky's 'complete divorce from the true demands of our time and a cult of fashion unworthy of talent'. Stravinsky had been publicly contemptuous of the Soviet state and its music. He insisted that nostalgia played no part in his decision to undertake the trip, which was opposed by many of his expatriate Russian friends. Instead he ascribed it to 'the evidence I have received' (from whom?) 'of a genuine desire or need for me by the younger generation of Russian musicians. No artist's name has been more abused in the Soviet Union than mine, but one cannot achieve the future we must achieve with the Russians by bearing a grudge.'

That nostalgia played an important part in his decision is confirmed, however, by the profound emotions it stirred in him. His face lit up with pleasure at seeing the Mariinsky Theatre again (now renamed the Kirov) and if he betrayed no emotion when revisiting the nearby building in which he had lived for the first twenty-four years of his life it was, as he told Craft, because 'I couldn't let myself'. For an eighty-year-old to encounter friends he had not seen for fifty years, to be welcomed by relatives that he had never met, to rehearse an orchestra in Russian for the first time in his life, must have revealed how very Russian he had remained despite a long and cosmopolitan exile. In an extraordinary impromptu speech after a dinner in his honour given by the Soviet Minister of Culture Yekaterina Furtseva, he regretted the circumstances that had made him an exile, lamented that he had not been able to take part in the fashioning of contemporary music in the Soviet Union, 'Yet the right to criticize Russia is mine, because Russia is mine and I love it, and I do not give any foreigner that right.' And in a curious inversion of that principle Stravinsky mixed on sociable terms with Khrennikov, who had often, to put it mildly, 'criticized' his music, and with Shostakovich, who had done so at least for public consumption.

During that same year, he also completed a brief anthem to words by T. S. Eliot and a short but complex 'musical play' for television, *The Flood*, wrote a substantial part of *Abraham and Isaac*, oversaw a slight revision of *The Nightingale*, completely recomposed the eight easy piano pieces ('The Five Fingers') of 1921 for an ensemble of

Les Noces: a scene from the 1966 revival at the Royal Opera House, Covent Garden, for which Bronislava Nijinska reproduced her original choreography, with sets and costumes closely based on those by Natalia Goncharova for the first production in 1923

fifteen instruments, made several recordings and published the third volume of his conversations with Robert Craft. It was Craft who was largely responsible for Stravinsky's ability to accept conducting engagements, upon which he depended for much of his income, well into his old age. Craft would rehearse the players in advance, often conducting part of the concert as well, to spare the energy of the increasingly frail composer.

Craft became a sort of surrogate son to Stravinsky and the old man a much loved second father to him. The composer's relationships with his real children were much less happy. During their early years he was much separated from them because of his need to travel; from 1921, the year his relationship with Vera began, he spent ever less time with them; and after the outbreak of war and his emigration to America he did not meet them for several years. Nevertheless his older son Theodore, a talented artist, and his surviving daughter Milène depended on him for financial support (Milène's French husband, André Marion, was for some years after the war Stravinsky's secretary, later his part-time accountant), while his younger son

Soulima's reputation as a pianist was due at least in part to the allure
of his surname. Stravinsky's published letters reveal a genuine love
and concern for his children, together with an impatient authorit-
arianism which distinctly recalls his description of his own father
(though Fyodor Stravinsky was 'remote' only in manner). By the time
that reunion between father and children was again possible after
the war Stravinsky had acquired a 'surrogate son' younger than any
of them.

This mixture of resentments and dependences was not likely to
cement a fragmented family. Stravinsky's children, because of their
father's hot temper, were more likely to approach him for money
through the intermediacy of the woman for whom he had 'abandoned' their mother. This cannot have helped matters, genuinely
though Vera seems to have liked her stepchildren. The ugliest chapter
of Stravinsky's life, all the uglier because it began in his eighty-seventh
year and did not end until eight years after his death, started with
the gift of some orange groves, purchased by Stravinsky as an invest-
ment, to (as he thought) his three children. The subsequent discovery
that the entire property had been transferred to Milène and André
Marion, Stravinsky's consequent mistrust of Marion (who only
returned a number of valuable manuscripts in his keeping when

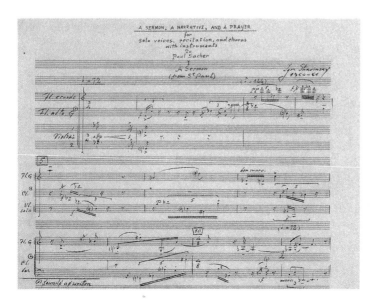

Autograph manuscript of
A Sermon, a Narrative and
a Prayer (1961)

threatened with legal action), his suspicion of his own lawyer (who had drawn up the transfer document for the orange groves), an attempt by that lawyer and the two younger Stravinsky children and their spouses to obtain access to a European bank account in the names of Igor and Vera Stravinsky, the law-suit after Stravinsky's death in which the three children of his first wife contested the right of his second to the property he had bequeathed her – all this makes distressing reading, and it seems at least possible that none of it would have occurred if Stravinsky's children had found him more approachable. None of them has published any account of their adult relationships with him, and of the correspondence between him and their mother only extracts from Catherine's letters have appeared, none of Stravinsky's own. If he felt guilt at his treatment of his children (and his daughter Milène, when he left Europe for the USA, was a gravely ill young woman in a sanatorium in soon-to-be occupied France) the vicious circle would have been a painful one for all concerned.

References to those children in the Stravinsky–Craft conversation-books are few and far between. The authenticity of the books, or at least their tone of voice, has occasionally been questioned. Craft himself fuelled controversy by publishing, in his *Stravinsky in Pictures and Documents* (of which Vera Stravinsky is named as co-author), a letter from the composer to his literary agent insisting that 'Bob … did write the book [*Conversations with Igor Stravinsky*, the first of the series]; it is his language, his presentation, his imagination, and his memory, and I am only protecting myself in not wanting it to appear as though I write or talk that way', adjacent to a statement of his own that 'Stravinsky *did* write the books, and most of the language, with its more foreign than English vocabulary, *was* his. The "presentation" was the work of the present writer.' By 1992 (in Craft's *Stravinsky: Glimpses of a Life*) this had been modified to 'much of the language of the books is mine'. Most of the autobiographical information in the books, however, could only have come from Stravinsky himself; the same is true of much of what is said about his own music, and the choice of subject must have been his most of the time (another case of it being well-nigh impossible to lead this horse to water). It is a pity, as Craft acknowledges, that Stravinsky's caution led to the deletion of some acidly expressed opinions, and that some of his spontaneity is inevitably lost; it is a pity too that one cannot always distinguish Stravinsky's venom and wit from Craft's.

The late serial works confirm the authenticity of the *Conversations'* remarks about serial practice and about those works of Schoenberg and his pupils that Stravinsky did or did not admire. It has also to be said that the sincerity of Stravinsky's 'conversion' is confirmed by the fact that it cost the intensely money-conscious old man a great deal: he pointed out in one of the Craft conversations that a recording of one of his 'post-*Rake*' works could be expected to sell about one-tenth as many copies as a 'new' *Firebird* or *Petrushka*; which is why he continued his more profitable conducting career until his eighty-fifth year; an important motive for publishing the conversation books was the welcome additional income they earned. His reverence for Webern is expressed not only in the conversations with Craft but in the very sound of *Movements* and the later Variations. Stravinsky praises Schoenberg's late, unfinished works for continuing 'to explore new ways and search for new laws' in the same paragraph as he dismisses Schoenberg's texts as 'appallingly bad, some of them so bad as to discourage performance'. Stravinsky's next three works continue to explore new ways of setting extremely good texts; they also continue his individual adaptation of serialism – 'searching for new laws' – to his own purposes.

A Sermon, a Narrative and a Prayer (1961) is an awkward title and its mingling of song with speech in the central section can be awkward in performance. This problem is still greater in *The Flood* (1962), where the concise eventfulness of the drama (a conflation, by Craft, of passages from the York and Chester cycles of mystery plays) led to a need for many passages of speech over music. Though in the 'Narrative' of the stoning of St Stephen, the sometimes-sung, sometimes-spoken vocal part and the bare instrumental lines may distract from one another, the initial 'Sermon' combines solemn choral writing with a demonstration that the fragmented style of *Movements* can be put to powerfully dramatic effect, recalling the energy of the Symphony in Three Movements (the two great eruptions at the words 'And our Lord is a consuming fire'). In the sombrely beautiful 'Prayer', to words by Thomas Dekker, Stravinsky finds yet another new and haunting sonority: for much of its length the singing is accompanied by a dark chiming from low harp and piano, pizzicato double basses and three gongs of different pitches.

The Flood owes much of its swift-moving alternation of choral chant, solo aria, instrumental numbers (intended to be danced) and folk comedy to the fact that it was designed for television, where changes of scene and focus can be instantaneous. The score, less than twenty-five minutes long, contains about fifteen individual numbers, of which the danced scenes of the building of the ark and the flood are by far the longest. Because it fits awkwardly into the repertories of opera houses and ballet companies (while needing the resources of both) and is hard to bring off in concert performance, it is very nearly Stravinsky's most rarely heard work. Yet it has considerable humour (Stravinsky, now the arch-serialist, uses chords containing all twelve pitches to represent 'chaos'; the choice of a square-dance 'caller' to beckon the animals into the ark is both clever and funny) and impressive solemnity (the voice of God given to two basses with sepulchral accompaniment for low strings and bass drum) to season its angular complexities.

Its successor, *Abraham and Isaac*, a 'sacred ballad' for baritone and chamber orchestra, is more difficult to approach and even more rarely performed. Stravinsky set the biblical story in Hebrew, as a 'gift' to the state of Israel after a particularly warm welcome there, and he directed that the text should never be sung in translation. Its musical language is no less esoteric, though here the problem is not, as in *Movements*, that the listener is bombarded with ideas more rapidly than can comfortably be absorbed on a single hearing. In *Abraham and Isaac* the soloist sings almost without pause, often to slender accompaniment, seldom 'dramatizing' the text in any way. It is like hearing a sacred text chanted by a cantor, the instruments reflecting on his ritual song with arcane commentaries. The beauty of some of these, the at times vehement and melismatic quality of the baritone's music are the keys to an enigmatic work which, by its very nature, may always remain rather secret.

Perhaps because sets of orchestral variations are among the master-pieces of both Schoenberg and Webern, Stravinsky next turned his attention to this form. The Variations are dedicated to the memory of Stravinsky's close friend Aldous Huxley, but he died when work on them was well advanced, so they are by no means conceived as a

Stravinsky's last visit to
London, September 1965:
rehearsing the Philharmonia
Orchestra at the Royal
Festival Hall for a concert
that was also televised

Stravinsky had already begun his last major work, the Requiem Canticles, by the time of the London concert of September 1965. He completed it a year later, in August 1966, at the age of eighty-four. He conducted his last recording session in January 1967, and his final concert in May of that year.

lament. They return to the epigrammatic terseness of *Movements*, but in still more laconic form. The fact that their theme is never stated gives the listener little help, and Stravinsky now extends patterning in twelves to matters of scoring and metre. Three of the variations (there are twelve of them, naturally, all extremely short: the entire work plays for less than five minutes) take the form of interludes for twelve instruments, each in a regular repeating pattern of bars consisting of 4+3+5(=12) beats. Each interlude consists of twelve simultaneous and independent melodic lines, scored respectively for twelve solo violins, ten violas with two double basses, and twelve wind instruments. Stravinsky described these sections as musical 'mobiles' whose apparent form would change on each hearing. In fact it would take a good many hearings to realize that they are identical (the lines are redistributed on each repetition, the first violin line in the first interlude reappearing in the next on the double bass – but now inverted – and so on), but they articulate the pared-down variation process very clearly, islands of mysteriously busy stasis amid bracingly angular counterpoint.

The major works of Stravinsky's last phase are punctuated by a series of far from minor but very brief 'occasional' pieces. All share the technical preoccupations of their contemporaries, but all have some feature which makes them more easily approachable; Stravinsky rations his strength but not his skill. The light-hearted *Greeting Prelude* is as genial a birthday tribute as could be wished, but it is also Stravinsky's very first quasi-serial orchestral work, and audibly a flexing of permutational muscle. The sober *Epitaphium*, a memorial to a generous patron, Prince Max Egon zu Fürstenberg, is simultaneously a tribute to Stravinsky's by now worshipped Webern (it is scored for the instrumental grouping of Webern's Songs Op. 15), an essay in neo-Webernian micro-structure (a series of seven 'responses' between a harp and a duet of flute and clarinet) and, in the harp part, a study for the deep chimings in the closing section of *A Sermon, a Narrative and a Prayer*.

The beautifully lyrical Double Canon for string quartet was written, rather puzzlingly, in memory of the painter Raoul Dufy. Stravinsky does not seem to have especially valued his work, the two never met, and in any case Dufy had been dead for six years when the piece was written. The impetus for the piece seems to have been an idea for two wind instruments, which Stravinsky later found capable of expansion into a double canon of sober grace as well as unusual strictness. A more uncompromising rigour is heard in the Anthem ('The dove descending breaks the air'), a setting of words from T. S. Eliot's 'Little Gidding', whose dry severity would perhaps have pleased the poet more than its impassive word-setting.

There is much more obviously personal feeling in *Elegy for J. F. K.* Stravinsky had met and liked John F. Kennedy, and a few months after the President's assassination he asked Auden for a simple lyric in his memory. Auden quite brilliantly sensed what Stravinsky would need and wrote four *haiku* (a Japanese verse-form in three lines totalling seventeen syllables), an ideal pretext for mingling formalized reserve and ritual lament, soberly scored for low voice and three clarinets. The tiny (thirty seconds long) *Fanfare for a New Theater*, written for the opening of the New York State Theater at the Lincoln Center (the new home of Balanchine's company), is a glittering two-

'When a just man dies, lamentation and praise, sorrow and joy are one'. Stravinsky admired and liked John F. Kennedy, and four months after the President's assassination asked W. H. Auden for 'a very quiet little lyric' that he could set to music in his memory.

part invention, likened by the Stravinsky scholar Eric Walter White to a pair of pennants 'flying and crackling in a brisk wind', and by Balanchine himself to two golden cockerels crowing at each other. The *Introitus* in memory of T. S. Eliot, finally, a setting of the opening section of the Latin Requiem Mass, combines the dark-coloured utterances of the voice of God from *The Flood* with the deep, chiming sonorities heard there and in *A Sermon, a Narrative and a Prayer*: the work is most impressively scored for male voices, harp, piano, drums and gongs, with a solo viola and double bass.

The gradual development of low-pitched chantings and sombre tollings in Stravinsky's late phase clearly predicts the sound-world of his last major composition, the Requiem Canticles of 1965/66. The *Introitus* and the Canticles, in response to their liturgical and funerary character, also mark the return of something largely absent in Stravinsky's work since *Movements*: obsessive repetition. Together with the chanting and tolling elements it gives a pronounced echo of the Russian Orthodox liturgy to these late works.

The Requiem Canticles were first planned as a short orchestral work, then expanded by the insertion of six epigrammatic extracts from the Requiem Mass. In the Prelude, for strings, urgent repeated notes support and punctuate four statements of a simple melody for solo violin, extra solo strings adding decorative counterpoints to each repetition. The 'Exaudi' has a dry five-note 'motto' for the harp, its austerity softened by a halo of flute, bassoon and string harmonics; the text is set briefly and very plainly, perhaps to point up by contrast the anguished shudder and stark cry that are the main substance of the 'Dies irae'. The 'Tuba mirum', its fanfare-like figures for two trumpets echoing settings of these words by Verdi and Berlioz, precedes an orchestral Interlude that was the first part of the work to be written and, according to Stravinsky, represents its 'formal lament'. Measured pairs of grave chords (a funeral march) punctuate brief interludes for wind instruments, the most extensive of them for four flutes; it strongly recalls both the Symphonies of Wind Instruments in memory of Debussy, written forty-seven years earlier, and Stravinsky's description of the lost Funeral Dirge for Rimsky-Korsakov, now fifty-nine years in the past: he recalled that his idea in that work had been to suggest the instruments of the orchestra filing past a tomb, each laying its own wreath of melody.

Patterns of repeated notes return to support the majestic four-part counterpoint of the 'Rex tremendae'. The 'Lacrimosa' is a floridly incantatory contralto solo, both strictly serial, indeed strictly 'rotatory', and a refraction of the 'Sektanskaya' that had ushered in Stravinsky's most Russian phase. In the 'Libera me' the sense of ancient ritual is intensified by shadowing the urgent chanting of four soloists with *sotto voce* mutterings from the chorus, like a congregation echoing the solemn ritual. The effect might have been still more marked had Stravinsky retained the original accompaniment, for harmonium; he substituted four horns at rehearsal. The work ends with a Postlude in which bright, clashing bell sounds (celesta, tubular bells and vibraphone) are interspersed between repetitions of a single, chiming chord for woodwind, piano, harp and horn. It has been called the 'chord of death'; it is also an obvious echo of *Les Noces* and thus a chord of rebirth.

Almost immediately after finishing the Requiem Canticles, as – in his phrase – 'a musical sigh of relief', Stravinsky began experimenting with the simple one-two-three rhythms of the first poem in English to be memorized by his wife on arrival in America. The rhythm suggested a melody, the melody combined with the metre of the poem to form a row, and thus rhythmic acuity and serial guile combined to set Edward Lear's *The Owl and the Pussy-cat* as Stravinsky's last work and his last musical tribute 'to Vera'. He attempted to begin other compositions during his remaining five years, but could not.

The last years of Stravinsky's life also produced a number of highly significant arrangements of works by other composers. He had no doubt been introduced to the ear-challengingly audacious dissonances of Carlo Gesualdo, Prince of Venosa (?1560–1613) by Craft, who had recruited a group of singers to perform Gesualdo's madrigals. ('Musician and murderer', as his first English biographers Cecil Gray and Philip Heseltine styled him, Gesualdo's notoriety for having ordered the murder of his wife and her lover – a crime for which his nobility exempted him from the death penalty – for long overshadowed his startling originality as a composer.) Stravinsky did not want any of his own earlier music to share the programme with the première of *Canticum sacrum* in St Mark's, Venice, in 1956. He suggested that it might be accompanied by Venetian sacred music

The Owl and the Pussy-Cat
(1966): Stravinsky's title
page, drawing and
dedication 'to Vera'

and, since he had recently acquired copies of the part-books for Gesualdo's *Sacrae cantiones* – several of which are incomplete – that he should re-construct one of them for this concert. The Venetian authorities demurred, apparently on the grounds that Gesualdo was not a Venetian, and the project was temporarily shelved.

Instead Stravinsky took Bach's canonic variations on the Christmas song 'Vom Himmel hoch' and freely arranged them as a companion work to the *Canticum*. He re-scored them for chorus and orchestra (the original is for organ), elaborately embellishing some of Bach's canons with additional counterpoints of his own. By enriching the third variation (of five) with especial ingenuity he also gave the work a structural similarity to his own piece. He retained the full German title of the work, using German also for its dedication (to Robert Craft) and an inscription on the manuscript referring to the 'liberties' he had taken: *mit Genehmigung des Meisters* ('with the Master's sanction').

Stravinsky had been too interested in the Gesualdo project to relinquish it, however, and he went on not only to supply the missing two voices in Gesualdo's 'Illumina nos' but to perform a similar service for two other incomplete motets, 'Da pacem, Domine' and 'Assumpta est Maria'. He did so quite freely, not so much assuming Gesualdo's style as adapting his own in homage. Two years later, for Gesualdo's quatercentenary in 1960, he took the same process rather further by 're-composing' three madrigals for chamber orchestra, discreetly outdoing the originals in harmonic asperity.

His two remaining arrangements, from the very end of his creative life, are a re-scoring of Sibelius's Canzonetta, Op. 62a, and an instrumentation of two songs by Hugo Wolf. The Sibelius, originally for string orchestra, was arranged for an octet of four horns, clarinet, bass clarinet, harp and double bass, partly as a gesture of gratitude for the award to Stravinsky of the Wihuri-Sibelius Prize, partly it would seem out of a nostalgia that the award from a Finnish foundation awoke in him. It is a rather Tchaikovskian piece, and Stravinsky liked its 'northern Italianate melodism … a part, and an attractive part, of St Petersburg culture'.

The two songs are both sombre, from the sacred lyrics in Wolf's Spanish Song-Book. They were scored in a single day, for voice and ten instruments, two years after the Requiem Canticles; according to

Stravinsky at eighty-eight,
in the last summer of his life,
at Evian-les-Bains on
Lake Geneva (photograph
by Mme Theodore
Strawinsky)

Craft Stravinsky 'wanted to say something about death and felt that
he could not compose anything of his own'.

His last years were saddened by the breach from his children and
punctuated by recurrences of grave illness. It seems almost incredible
that a man who could no longer compose and was often seriously
ill should have continued conducting until not long before his eighty-
fifth birthday. From that point on, his undiminished intellectual
vigour had to occupy itself with reading and, above all, with listening.
In the foreword to the last of his conversation books he said: 'It is
almost five years now since I have completed an original composition,
a time during which I have had to transform myself from a composer

to a listener. The vacuum which this left has not been filled, but I have been able to live with it, thanks, in the largest measure, to the music of Beethoven ... I am thankful that I can listen to and love the music of other men in a way I could not do when I was composing my own.'

Stravinsky spent numerous periods in hospital during his last few years. His increasing frailty led to a move in the autumn of 1969 to a New York apartment and to a plan, never realized, to 'retire' to Paris or its outskirts. He was severely ill the following spring but well enough to convalesce at Evian, on the French shore of Lake Geneva. Back in New York he was ill again the following March, so ill that, not for the first time, doctors did not expect him to recover. Discharged, he moved into a new apartment, recently purchased by his wife. Four days later, scribbling a brief note in Russian, he mistakenly signed his name in Latin script. Vera asked him to add a signature in Cyrillic but instead, knowing that she was watching, wrote, 'Oh, how I love you!'. Four days later still, after a final crisis, he died, two and a half months before his eighty-ninth birthday, on 6 April 1971. A Russian Orthodox funeral service took place on the 9th, Good Friday, and in Venice on the 15th, after a Greek Orthodox Mass in the church of SS. Giovanni e Paolo (the service incorporating a performance of the Requiem Canticles), he was buried on the island cemetery of S. Michele, in the section reserved for those of the Orthodox faith, next to the grave of Serge Diaghilev.

He had exerted a profound influence on music for sixty years. His expansion of the role of rhythm was one of the great turning-points in musical history, and it affected even composers whose paths diverged widely from his own. Pierre Boulez not only acknowledged the importance for him of Stravinsky's rhythmic innovations, but pointed out how crucial they were for his own teacher Olivier Messiaen. Stravinsky's other most obvious legacy, his neo-classicism or rather his attitude to the past, best expressed in a couple of sentences from his *Chronicles of my Life* – 'In borrowing a form already established and consecrated, the creative artist is not in the least restricting the manifestations of his personality. On the contrary, it is more detached, and stands out better, when it moves within the limits of a convention.' – has been more contentious. For a modernist like Boulez this is a fatal compromise, a failure to move forward from

Stravinsky's funeral,
SS Giovanni e Paolo, Venice,
15 April 1971

The Rite of Spring, a preoccupation with 'style'. It was nevertheless extremely influential, on most French composers between the two World Wars, on most American composers born between 1900 and the Second World War and on many others, not only of the younger generation: the impact of Stravinsky's neo-classicism on the later music of Manuel de Falla was profound.

The most fruitful effect of influence is of course on the work of composers for whom it unlocks a strong personal voice. This was true for Aaron Copland, Edgard Varèse and Francis Poulenc, inevitably less so for the minor members of the École de Paris or the less talented worshippers at Nadia Boulanger's église. It is unlikely that the explorations of rhythm following *The Rite of Spring* can continue much further; the more obvious aspects of neo-classicism seem also worked out. Whether Stravinsky's influence will continue perhaps depends on a realization of how much more there is to his style than neo-classicism and a virtuoso use of asymmetric rhythm. The Belgian composer Henri Pousseur has examined the implications of Stravinskian harmony in two overt homages, *L'effacement du Prince Igor* and *Stravinsky au futur*; Stravinsky's exploration of musical theatre and his abrupt juxtapositions of material in works such as the Symphonies of Wind Instruments have both fruitfully affected the music of Sir Harrison Birtwistle. Stravinsky's attitude to the past was approvingly quoted (and re-named 'vampirism') by Robin Holloway when discussing his own re-use of – among others – Schumann. Perhaps Stravinsky's ability in old age to re-make his language while remaining himself, and at the same time to create sounds that are arrestingly new, is the best possible influence. As Pierre Boulez put it, in fact in reference to the *Canticum sacrum*, though I would extend it to Stravinsky's work as a whole: 'Where a host of others have continued to stammer and to pontificate, to chatter and to prejudge, to mince round issues or to skimp them, to rage, to threaten, to mock and to torpedo, Stravinsky has simply acted.'

Classified List of Works

Dates in brackets are those of composition. With rare stated exceptions 'fp' indicates the date of the first public performance; a few works, mainly juvenilia and occasional pieces where no performance details are known, are marked 'fp?'. Entries within square brackets are arrangements of music by other composers. Titles are given first in their most familiar form, followed by others in current use. Concert suites from ballets, etc. are not duplicated under 'Orchestral Music', but for the sake of clarity certain transcriptions or recompositions, often with altered titles, are listed both in their original and in their later form. For vocal works, the language of the text set by Stravinsky is indicated (except for those with words by English or American writers, which he invariably set in English), though editions of many of his Russian works included, with his approval, singing translations in other languages.

Stage Works

The Nightingale (Solovey, Le Rossignol), 'lyric tale' in three acts for soloists, chorus and orchestra, Russian libretto by Stravinsky and Stepan Mitusov after Hans Christian Andersen (1908–9 and 1913–14). fp Paris, 26 May 1914. Arranged as *The Song of the Nightingale* (Pyesnya Solov'ya, Le Chant du rossignol), symphonic poem for orchestra (see below).

[Grieg: *Kobold,* transcribed for orchestra for the ballet *Les Orientales* (1910). Unpublished.
fp Paris 19 May 1909]

[Chopin: Nocturne in A flat and Valse brillante in E flat, transcribed for orchestra for the ballet *Les Sylphides* (1909). fpp Paris, 2 June 1909]

The Firebird (Zhar'ptitsa, L'Oiseau de feu), ballet in two scenes for large orchestra (1909–10). fp Paris, 25 June 1910. Concert suites: (a) 1911; (b) 1919 (for reduced orchestra); 1945 (as 1919 but with extra music).

Petrushka, ballet in four scenes for large orchestra (1910–11). fp Paris, 13 June 1911. Revised version for reduced orchestra (1946). 'Three Movements from *Petrushka'* transcribed for piano (see below).

The Rite of Spring (Vesna svyashchennaya, Le Sacre du printemps), 'scenes of pagan Russia' in two parts, for large orchestra (1911–13). fp Paris, 29 May 1913. Transcription for piano duet (1913). Revision of 'Sacrificial Dance' (1943).

[Mussorgsky: *Khovanshchina,* one aria orchestrated and final scene completed (1913). fp Paris, 5 June 1913]

Renard (Bayka), 'burlesque to be sung and acted' for four male voices and fifteen instruments, words traditional Russian (1916). fp Paris, 18 May 1922

Les Noces (Svadebka, The Wedding), 'Russian choreographic scenes' in four tableaux for four soloists, chorus, four pianos and percussion, words traditional Russian (1914–17, final scoring 1923). fp Paris, 13 June 1923

The Soldier's Tale (L'Histoire du soldat), 'to be read, played and danced', in two parts, for three actors, dancer and seven players, words (in French) C. F. Ramuz (1918). fp Lausanne, 28 September 1918. Suites: (a) for the original ensemble of seven players (1920); (b) for violin, clarinet and piano (1919).

[Mussorgsky: *Boris Godunov,* arrangement of a chorus from the Prologue for piano (1918). Unpublished. fp?]

Pulcinella, 'ballet with song' in one act, for soprano, tenor, bass and chamber orchestra, text (in Italian) and music after Pergolesi (1919–20). fp Paris, 15 May 1920. Suites: (a) for chamber orchestra (1920); (b) for violin and piano (1925); (c) *Suite italienne* for cello and piano and (d) for violin and piano (see below).

[Tchaikovsky: *The Sleeping Beauty,* orchestration of Aurora's variation and Act II entr'acte (1921). Unpublished. fp London, 2 November 1921]

Mavra, 'opera buffa' in one act, for soloists and orchestra, libretto (in Russian) by Boris Kochno after Pushkin (1921–2). fp Paris, 3 June 1922

Oedipus Rex, 'opera-oratorio' in two acts, for speaker, soloists, chorus and orchestra, libretto by Jean Cocteau after Sophocles, translated into Latin by Jean Daniélou, with narration to be spoken in the language of the audience (1926–7). fp Paris, 30 May 1927

Apollo (Apollon musagète), ballet in two scenes, for string orchestra (1927–8). fp Washington DC, 27 April 1928

The Fairy's Kiss (Le Baiser de la fée), 'allegorical ballet' in four scenes, for orchestra, after Tchaikovsky (1928). fp Paris, 27 November 1928. Suites: 'Divertimento' (see below).

Persephone (Perséphone), 'melodrama' in three scenes, for speaker (woman's voice), tenor, chorus and orchestra, words (in French) by André Gide (1933–4). fp Paris, 30 April 1934

Jeu de cartes (A Card Game), 'ballet in three deals', for orchestra (1935–6). fp New York, 27 April 1937

[Tchaikovsky: *The Sleeping Beauty,* transcription of 'Bluebird' *pas de deux* for small orchestra (1941). fp?]

Circus Polka, for wind band (1942). fp New York, spring 1942. Version for symphony orchestra (1942). fp Cambridge, Massachusetts, 13 January 1944

Scènes de ballet, for orchestra (1944). fp Philadelphia, 1944

Orpheus, ballet in three scenes, for orchestra (1946–7). fp New York, 28 April 1948

The Rake's Progress, opera in three acts, for soloists, chorus and orchestra, libretto by W. H. Auden and Chester Kallman (1947–51). fp Venice, 11 September 1951. Arrangement of Lullaby ('Gently, little boat') for two recorders made for Perry Neuschatz, an architect and amateur recorder player, who had designed an extension to the Stravinskys' house.

Agon, 'ballet for twelve dancers', for orchestra (1953–7). fp Los Angeles, 17 June 1957

The Flood, 'musical play' for soloists, speakers, chorus and orchestra, words (in English) by Robert Craft, after the Bible and the York and Chester mystery plays (1961–2). fp 14 June 1962 (CBS television broadcast)

Fanfare for a New Theater, for two trumpets (1964). fp New York, 19 April 1964

Piano
(including piano duet, two pianos and pianola)

Tarantella, for piano (1898). Unpublished. fp?

Scherzo, for piano (1902). fp?

Piano Sonata in F sharp minor (1903–4). fp St Petersburg, 1905

Four Studies, Op. 7, for piano (1908). fp St Petersburg (?), 1908

Valse des fleurs, for piano duet, easy left-hand part (1914). Unpublished. fp New York, 1949

Three Easy Pieces, for piano duet, easy left-hand part (1914). fp Lausanne, 8 November 1919. Transcribed for small orchestra as Nos. 1–3 of Suite No. 2 (see below).

Souvenir d'une marche boche, for piano (1915). Written for an anthology sold in aid of Belgian orphans. fp?

Valse pour les enfants, for piano (1916–17). Written for the newspaper *Le Figaro.* fp?

Five Easy Pieces, for piano duet, easy right-hand part (1916–17). fp Lausanne, 8 November 1919. Transcribed for orchestra, Nos. 1–4 as Suite No. 1, No. 5 as finale of Suite No. 2 (see below).

Study, for pianola (1917). fp London, 13 October 1921. Transcribed for orchestra as No. 4 of Four Studies (see below).

Piano-Rag-Music, for piano (1919). fp Lausanne, 8 November 1919

Three Movements from *Petrushka* (see above) transcribed for piano (1921). fp?

Les Cinq Doigts ('The Five Fingers'), for piano (1921). fp? Transcribed for fifteen instruments as Eight Instrumental Miniatures (see below).

Sonata, for piano (1924). fp Donaueschingen, July 1925

Serenade in A, for piano (1925). fp Frankfurt am Main, 25 November 1925

Concerto, for two solo pianos (1932–5). fp Paris, 21 November 1935

Sonata, for two pianos (1943–4). fp Madison, Wisconsin, July 1944

Vocal

Storm-Cloud, song for voice and piano, words (in Russian) by Pushkin (1902). fp?

Cantata for Rimsky-Korsakov's Sixtieth Birthday, for chorus and piano (1904). Lost. fp (private) 19 March 1904, at Rimsky-Korsakov's apartment in St Petersburg.

How the Mushrooms Prepared for War, song for bass voice and piano, words traditional Russian (1904). fp?

Conductor and Tarantula, song for voice and piano, Russian words by 'Kozma Prutkov' (pseudonym of Aleksey Tolstoy and others) (1906). Lost. fp (private) 19 March 1904, at Rimsky-Korsakov's apartment in St Petersburg

Faun and Shepherdess (Favn i Pastushka, Faune et bergère), Op. 2, suite for mezzo-soprano and orchestra, words (in Russian) by Pushkin (1906–7). fp St Petersburg, 16 February 1908

Pastorale, for (wordless) soprano and piano (1907). Arranged for soprano and four wind instruments (1923) and, somewhat expanded, for violin and piano or for violin and four wind instruments (1933). fp (first version) St Petersburg, winter 1908

Two Songs, Op. 6, for mezzo-soprano and piano, words (in Russian) by S. Gorodetsky (1907–8). fp St Petersburg, winter 1908

[*The Song of the Flea*: (a) by Beethoven, (b) by Mussorgsky, both arranged for bass voice and orchestra (1909), words by Goethe in Russian translation. fpp St Petersburg 1910]

Two Poems of Verlaine, Op. 9, for baritone and piano (1910), text set in French. fp? Revised and transcribed for baritone and orchestra (1953).

Two poems of Balmont, for high voice and piano (1911), text in Russian. fp? Revised and transcribed for soprano and small orchestra (1955).

Zvezdoliki (Le Roi des étoiles, The King of the Stars), for male chorus and large orchestra, words (in Russian) by Konstantin Balmont (1911). fp Brussels, 19 April 1939

Three Japanese Lyrics (Trois Poésies de la lyrique japonaise), for soprano and piano or chamber orchestra, words anon. Japanese (1912–13). fp Paris, 14 January 1914. NB: the published score prints the texts in Russian, French, German and English, but Stravinsky's sketches indicate that he originally considered setting them in Japanese.

Three Little Songs ('Recollections of my Childhood'), for voice and piano, Russian words by Stravinsky (1913). fp? Revised and transcribed for voice and small orchestra (1929–30).

Pribaoutki (Chansons plaisantes), for voice and eight instruments, words traditional Russian (1914). fp Vienna, 6 June 1919

Cat's Cradle Songs (Berceuses du chat), for contralto and three clarinets, words traditional Russian (1915). fp Vienna, 6 June 1919

Four Russian Peasant Songs (Podblyudnïya: 'Saucers'), for women's voices, words traditional Russian (1914–17). fp Geneva, 1917. Revised for women's voices and four horns (1954)

Three Tales for Children, for voice and piano, words traditional Russian (1916–17). fp? No. 1 revised and transcribed for voice and orchestra (1923), Nos. 2 and 3 transcribed for voice, flute, harp and guitar as Nos. 3 and 4 of Four Songs (see below).

Berceuse, for voice and piano, Russian words by Stravinsky (1917). fp?

Four Russian Songs, for voice and piano, words traditional Russian (1918–19). fp? Nos. 1 and 4 transcribed as Nos. 1 and 2 of Four Songs (see below).

Pater noster (Oche nash') for chorus (1924), words in Slavonic. fp? Version with Latin text (1949).

Symphony of Psalms (Symphonie de Psaumes), for chorus and orchestra (1930), text from the Bible, in Latin. fp Brussels, 13 December 1930

Credo (Simbol' vyerï), for chorus (1932), words in Slavonic. fp? Version with Latin text (1957).

Ave Maria (Bogoroditse dyevo), for chorus (1934), words in Slavonic. fp? Version with Latin text (1949).

Petit Ramusianum harmonique, for solo voice (speaking and singing), words (in French) by Charles-Albert Cingria (1937). fp?

Babel, cantata for narrator, male voice chorus and orchestra (1944), words from the Bible, in English. (Part of collaborative suite 'Genesis'). fp Los Angeles, 18 November 1945

Petit Canon pour la fête de Nadia Boulanger, for two tenors, words (in French) by Jean de Meung (1947). fp?

Mass, for chorus and double wind quintet (1944–8), text set in Latin. fp Milan, 27 October 1948

Cantata, for soprano, tenor, women's chorus and five instruments, words anon. English XV and XVI century (1951–2). fp Los Angeles, 11 November 1952

Three Songs from William Shakespeare, for mezzo-soprano, flute, clarinet and viola (1953). fp Los Angeles, 8 March 1954

In memoriam Dylan Thomas, 'dirge canons and song' for tenor, string quartet and four trombones, words by Dylan Thomas (1954). fp Los Angeles, 20 September 1954

Four Songs, for voice, flute, harp and guitar (1955), transcribed from Nos. 1 and 4 of Four Russian Songs, and Nos. 1 and 2 of Three Tales for Children (see above). fp Los Angeles, 21 February 1955

Canticum sacrum ad honorem Sancti Marci nominis, for tenor, baritone, chorus and orchestra (1955), words from the Bible, set in Latin. fp Venice, 13 September 1956

[Bach: Chorale Variations on 'Vom Himmel hoch', transcription and arrangement for chorus and orchestra (1955–6), text in German. fp Ojai, California, 27 May, 1956]

[*Tres sacrae cantiones*, by Gesualdo: completed for six and seven voices, words in Latin (1957–9). fp?]

Threni: id est Lamentationes Jeremiae prophetae, for six soloists, chorus and orchestra (1957–8), texts, in Latin, from the Bible. fp Venice, 23 September 1958

A Sermon, a Narrative and a Prayer, for alto and tenor, speaker, chorus and orchestra, English text from the Bible and Thomas Dekker (1960–61). fp Basel, 23 February 1962

Anthem ('The dove descending breaks the air'), for chorus, words T. S. Eliot (1961–2). fp Los Angeles, 19 February 1962

Abraham and Isaac, 'sacred ballad' for baritone and chamber orchestra, words from the Bible (1962–3), text in Hebrew. fp Jerusalem, 23 August 1964

Elegy for J. F. K., for medium voice and three clarinets, words W. H. Auden (1964). fp Los Angeles, 6 April 1964

Introitus T. S. Eliot in memoriam, for men's chorus and chamber ensemble, Latin words from the Requiem Mass (1965). fp Chicago, 17 April 1965

Requiem Canticles, for contralto and bass, chorus and orchestra, Latin words from the Requiem Mass (1965–6). fp Princeton University, 8 October 1966

The Owl and the Pussy-Cat, for soprano and piano, words Edward Lear (1966). fp Los Angeles, 31 October 1966

[Hugo Wolf: Two Sacred Songs, transcribed for mezzo-soprano and ten instruments (1969), texts anon. Spanish, in German translations by Paul Heyse and Emanuel Geibel. fp Los Angeles, 6 September 1968]

Orchestral

(including jazz band and large instrumental ensemble)

Symphony in E flat, for orchestra, Op. 1 (1905–7). fp St Petersburg, 22 January 1908

Scherzo fantastique, Op. 3, for orchestra (1907–8). fp St Petersburg, 6 February 1909

Fireworks, Op. 4, for orchestra (1908). fp St Petersburg, 6 February 1909

Chant funèbre, Op. 5, for wind instruments (1908, in memory of Rimsky-Korsakov). Lost. fp St Petersburg, autumn 1908

The Song of the Nightingale (Pyesnya Solovya, Le Chant du rossignol), symphonic poem for orchestra (1916–17), derived from parts of Acts I and II of the 'lyric tale' *The Nightingale* (see above). fp Geneva, 6 December 1919

Four Studies, for orchestra (1914–18), transcribed from the Study for pianola (see above) and the Three Pieces for string quartet (see below). fp Berlin, 7 November 1930

Symphonies of Wind Instruments (Symphonies d'instruments à vent), for twenty-three wind players (1920). fp London, 10 June 1921. Revised and rescored (1947).

Concerto, for piano, wind instruments, timpani and double basses (1923–4). fp Paris, 22 May 1924

Suite No. 1, for small orchestra (1917–25), transcribed from the first four of the Five Easy Pieces for piano duet (see above). fp Paris, spring 1921 (as incidental music to a revue sketch)

Suite No. 2, for small orchestra (1921), transcribed from the Three Easy Pieces and the last of the Five Easy Pieces for piano duet (see above). fp?

Capriccio, for piano and orchestra (1928–9). fp Paris,
6 December 1929

Concerto in D, for violin and orchestra (1931).
fp Berlin, 23 October 1931

Divertimento, symphonic suite for orchestra (1934),
drawn from the 'allegorical ballet' *The Fairy's Kiss*
(Le Baiser de la fée) (see above; NB change of title). fp?

Praeludium, for jazz ensemble (1936–7). fp Los Angeles,
18 October 1953

'Dumbarton Oaks' – Concerto in E flat, for chamber
orchestra (1937–8). fp Washington DC, 8 May 1938

Symphony in C, for orchestra (1938–40). fp Chicago,
7 November 1940

[John Stafford Smith: *The Star-Spangled Banner*,
transcription for orchestra (1941). fp Los Angeles,
14 October 1941]

Danses concertantes, for chamber orchestra (1940–42).
fp Los Angeles, 8 February 1942

Four Norwegian Moods, for orchestra (1942).
fp Cambridge, Massachusetts, 13 January 1944

Ode, 'elegiacal chant' in three parts, for orchestra
(1943). fp Boston, 8 October 1943

Scherzo à la russe, for jazz band (1944). fp Hollywood,
1944 (radio broadcast). Transcription for orchestra
(1943–4). fp San Francisco, March 1946

Symphony in Three Movements, for orchestra
(1942–5). fp New York, 24 January 1946

Ebony Concerto, for clarinet and jazz band (1945).
fp New York, 25 March 1946

Concerto in D, for string orchestra (1946). fp Basel,
27 January 1947

Greeting Prelude, for orchestra (1955). fp Boston,
4 April 1955

Movements, for piano and orchestra (1958–9).
fp New York, 10 January 1960

Eight Instrumental Miniatures, for fifteen players
(1962), transcribed and recomposed from
Les Cinq Doigts for piano (see above). fp Toronto,
29 April 1962

Variations Aldous Huxley in memoriam, for orchestra
(1963–4). fp Chicago, 17 April 1965

Chamber/Instrumental

Three Pieces, for string quartet (1914). fp Chicago, 8
November 1915. Transcribed for orchestra as Nos. 1–3
of Four Studies (see above)

Canons, for two horns (1917). Written for a doctor
(and amateur horn-player) who had treated Stravinsky's
daughter Lyudmila for a serious attack of appendicitis.
Unpublished, the manuscript presumed lost. fp?

Lied ohne Name, for two bassoons (1918?). fp?

Ragtime, for eleven instruments (1917–18). fp London,
27 April 1920. Transcribed for solo piano (1919)

Three Pieces, for clarinet solo (1918). Written for
Werner Reinhart, a Swiss patron of the arts and an
amateur clarinettist, who had sponsored several
concerts of Stravinsky's music and the first production
of *The Soldier's Tale*. fp Lausanne, 8 November 1919

[*La Marseillaise*: arrangement for solo violin (1919).
Unpublished. fp?]

Concertino, for string quartet (1920). fp New
York, 3 November 1920. Transcribed for twelve
instruments (1953).

Octet, for wind instruments (1922–3). fp Paris,
18 October 1923

Divertimento, for violin and piano (1932), transcribed
by Stravinsky and S. Dushkin from *The Fairy's Kiss*
(Le Baiser de la fée, see above). fp?

Duo concertant, for violin and piano (1932). fp Berlin,
28 October 1932

Suite italienne, (a) for cello and piano (1932)
transcribed by Stravinsky and Gregor Piatigorsky; (b)
for violin and piano (1933?) transcribed by Stravinsky
and Samuel Dushkin; both based on music from the
ballet *Pulcinella* (see above). fpp?

Tango, for piano or voice and piano (1940). fp?
Transcription for instrumental ensemble (1953). fp Los
Angeles, 18 October 1953

Elegy, for solo viola or violin (1944). fp Washington
DC, 26 January 1945

Septet, for clarinet, bassoon, horn, string trio and
piano (1952–3). fp Dumbarton Oaks (Washington
DC), 23 January 1954

*Epitaphium 'Fur das Grabmal des Prinzen Max Egon
zu Fürstenberg'*, for flute, clarinet and harp (1959). fp
Donaueschingen, 17 October 1959

Double Canon, 'Raoul Dufy in memoriam', for string
quartet (1959). fp New York, 20 December 1959

[*Monumentum pro Gesualdo di Venosa (ad CD annum)*:
three Gesualdo madrigals recomposed for instruments
(1960). fp Venice, 27 September 1960]

[Canzonetta for strings Op. 62a, by Sibelius:
transcription for eight instruments (1963). fp Helsinki,
22 March 1964]

Further Reading

With the reservations already mentioned, the most important sources of information on Stravinsky's life and work are his own writings, generally written in collaboration with others, and those of his close musical associate Robert Craft. A list of these follows, and then a selective annotated list of other books, generally of value for their detailed analysis of the music.

Stravinsky, I. *Chroniques de ma vie* (Paris, Denoël Steele, 1935/6); in English as *Chronicles of My Life* (London, Gollancz; New York, Simon and Schuster, 1936)

Poétique musicale (Cambridge, Mass., Harvard University Press, 1942); in English as *The Poetics of Music* (London, Gollancz; New York, Simon and Schuster, 1947)

Stravinsky, I., and R. Craft *Conversations with Igor Stravinsky* (London, Faber; New York, Doubleday, 1959)

Memories and Commentaries (London, Faber; New York, Doubleday 1960)

Expositions and Developments (London, Faber; New York, Doubleday 1962)

Dialogues and a Diary (New York, Doubleday, 1963; London, Faber, 1968). Subsequently reissued without the extracts from Robert Craft's diary as *Dialogues*

Themes and Conclusions (London, Faber, 1972). A one-volume revised conflation of *Themes and Episodes* (New York, Knopf, 1966) and *Retrospectives and Conclusions* (New York, Knopf, 1969), again omitting extracts from Craft's diaries, some of which reappeared in the following:

Craft, R. *Stravinsky: the Chronicle of a Friendship, 1948–1971* (New York, Knopf; London, Gollancz, 1972)

ed: *Stravinsky: Selected Correspondence* (3 vols., London, Faber, 1982, 1984, 1985)

Igor and Vera Stravinsky: a Photograph Album (London, Thames and Hudson, 1982)

A Stravinsky Scrapbook, 1940–1971 (London, Thames and Hudson, 1983)

Dearest Bubushkin: Selected Letters and Diaries of Vera and Igor Stravinsky (London, Thames and Hudson, 1985)

Stravinsky: Glimpses of a Life (London, Lime Tree, 1992)

Stravinsky, V., and R. Craft *Stravinsky in Pictures and Documents* (New York, Simon & Schuster, 1978; London, Hutchinson, 1979)

Asafyev, B. *A Book about Stravinsky* (translated by Richard French; Ann Arbor, Michigan, UMI Research Press, 1982). First published in Russia in 1929 and almost immediately suppressed, this was for many years the only attempt at a Russian perspective on Stravinsky. Especially valuable on the Russian roots of Stravinsky's style; very perceptive in its discussions of such key works as *Renard* and *Les Noces*.

Ledermann, M. ed: *Stravinsky in the Theater* (New York, Pellegrini and Cudahy, 1949; London, Peter Owen, 1951). Out-of-date, and the 1975 re-issue by Da Capo Press is a photographic reprint, not a revision, but it contains many essays on Stravinsky's work by his contemporaries and collaborators that are not accessible elsewhere.

Schönberger, E. and L. Andriessen *Het apollinisch uurwerk* (Amsterdam, De Bezige Bij, 1983; translated by Jeff Hamburg as *The Apollonian Clockwork*, Oxford University Press, 1989). A non-chronological, anti-analytical montage of unconventional and unexpected perspectives on Stravinsky. Oustandingly imaginative, often witty, throughout compulsively readable and provocative.

Schouvaloff, A. and V. Borovsky *Stravinsky on Stage* (London, Stainer and Bell, 1982). A catalogue, very richly illustrated, of all Stravinsky's works for the stage, including details of important later productions and a list of his concert works that have been choreographed.

van den Toorn, P. *The Music of Igor Stravinsky* (New Haven, Yale University Press, 1983). Accessible only to the reader with an advanced command of the language of musical analytical theory, the book is of great importance for its fundamental study of Stravinsky's harmony and pitch organization.

Vlad, R. *Stravinsky* (second edition: Oxford University Press, 1967). A most intelligent and thought-provoking study of Stravinsky's entire output, with the exception only of the very late works. The third edition (Turin, Einaudi, 1983) repairs these omissions handsomely, and has been exhaustively revised, but not yet translated into English.

Walsh, S. *The Music of Igor Stravinsky* (London and New York, Routledge, 1988). For the reader with some knowledge of musical terminology the most thoughtful and comprehensive study of Stravinsky's music yet published. Much of the analysis is new and exceptionally enlightening.

White, E. W. *Stravinsky: the Composer and His Works* (second edition: London, Faber, 1979). An extremely detailed and critically sound catalogue of Stravinsky's works, in chronological order, with very full discussions of their genesis, musical features and first performances; the preliminary biographical study is extensive and there are useful appendices.

Selective Discography

Stravinsky was the first great composer to leave a
substantial recorded legacy of his own works. He made
recordings, as pianist and conductor, over a period of
forty years, most intensively after the arrival of the
long-playing record when John McClure of
Columbia/CBS made a determined effort to record
most of Stravinsky's major works, under the composer's
direction, in the new medium. All these recordings
were remastered and reissued for Stravinsky's centenary
in 1982 and have since, in somewhat amplified form,
reappeared on CD as the 'Igor Stravinsky Edition',
from Sony Classical, the successor of Columbia/CBS.
The edition is available as a boxed set of twenty-two
CDs, and was originally also issued in twelve separate
volumes, mostly of two CDs each. At the time of
writing only the complete twenty-two-CD set and four
of its constituent volumes are available: Vols. 1 and 2
(the ballet scores), Vol. 4 (the symphonies) and Vol. 9
(*The Rake's Progress*). Sony have plans to reissue the
remaining eight volumes, devoted to Vol. 3 (ballet
suites), Vol. 5 (concertos), Vol. 6 ('miniature
masterpieces'), Vol. 7 (chamber music and historical
recordings), Vol. 8 (*The Nightingale, Mavra* and thirty-
three songs), Vol. 10 (oratorio and melodrama), Vol. 11
(sacred works) and Vol. 12 (recordings conducted by
Robert Craft under Stravinsky's supervision).

Stravinsky's own performances have a remarkable
fire and precision as well as unique authority; in
remastered form his accounts of *The Rite of Spring, The
Rake's Progress* and *Agon*, for example, can bear
comparison with all but the very finest of more recent
recordings. But many of them are in mono – some
rather drily and clinically recorded – and with certain
later works the performances are sometimes by artists
more notable for their accuracy than for their beauty of
sound. The importance of Stravinsky's own recordings,
however, cannot be exaggerated, and the list of other

recordings which follows is selected on two criteria:
that the performance should be at least as good as
Stravinsky's own, and the recording should be better.
Minor works and most of his transcriptions of other
composers' music are omitted. Where a major work
does not appear in this discography it is either because
Stravinsky's own recording strikes me as unsurpassed
(e.g., *The Rake's Progress*) or where no satisfactory
recording (e.g., *Mavra*) currently exists.

Stage Works

The Nightingale
Phyllis Bryn-Julson, Ian Caley, Neil Howlett;
BBC Singers and Symphony Orchestra conducted
by Pierre Boulez.
ERATO 2292–45627–2

The Firebird
City of Birmingham Symphony Orchestra conducted
by Sir Simon Rattle; with Stravinsky's *Scherzo à la russe*
and Four Studies
EMI CDC7 49178–2

Petrushka
Berlin Philharmonic Orchestra conducted by
Bernard Haitink; with Stravinsky's *Scènes de ballet*
PHILIPS 422 415–2PH

The Rite of Spring
London Philharmonic Orchestra conducted by
Sir Charles Mackerras; with Stravinsky's *Fireworks,
Circus Polka* and *Greeting Prelude*
EMI EMINENCE CD–EMX 2188

The Rite of Spring
City of Birmingham Symphony Orchestra conducted
by Sir Simon Rattle; with Stravinsky's *Apollo*
EMI CDC7 49636–2

Renard
Various soloists; Matrix Ensemble conducted by
Robert Ziegler; with works by Falla and Milhaud
ASV CDDCA 758

Les Noces
Various soloists; English Bach Festival Percussion
Ensemble conducted by Leonard Bernstein; with
Stravinsky's Mass
DG 423 251–2GC

The Soldier's Tale
Aage Haugland (speaker); members of Royal Scottish
National Orchestra conducted by Neeme Järvi
CHANDOS CHAN 9189

Pulcinella
Ann Murray (mezzo-soprano), Anthony Rolfe
Johnson (tenor), Simon Estes (bass); Ensemble
InterContemporain conducted by Pierre Boulez; with
Stravinsky's *The Song of the Nightingale*
ERATO 2292–45382–2

Oedipus Rex
Jean Desailly (speaker), Vera Soukupová (mezzo-
soprano), Ivo Zídek (tenor); Czech Philharmonic
Chorus and Orchestra conducted by Karel Ančerl;
with Stravinsky's Symphony of Psalms
SUPRAPHON 11 1947–2

Apollo
City of Birmingham Symphony Orchestra
conducted by Sir Simon Rattle; with Stravinsky's
The Rite of Spring
EMI CDC7 49636–2

The Fairy's Kiss
Royal Scottish National Orchestra conducted by
Neeme Järvi; with Tchaikovsky (arr. Stravinsky)
'Bluebird' *pas de deux* from *The Sleeping Beauty*
CHANDOS CHAN 8360

Persephone
Anne Fournet (speaker), Anthony Rolfe Johnson
(tenor); London Philharmonic Choir and Orchestra
conducted by Kent Nagano; with Stravinsky's *The Rite
of Spring*
VIRGIN CLASSICS VCK7 59077

Jeu de cartes
Orpheus
Royal Concertgebouw Orchestra conducted by Neeme
Järvi
CHANDOS CHAN 9014

Piano

Concerto for Two Solo Pianos
Sonata for Two Pianos
Vladimir Ashkenazy and Andrei Gavrilov (pianos);
with Stravinsky's transcriptions for two pianos or piano
duet of *Scherzo à la russe* and *The Rite of Spring*
DECCA 433 829–2DH

Three Easy Pieces
Five Easy Pieces
Concerto for Two Solo Pianos
Sonata for Two Pianos
Alfons and Aloys Kontarsky (pianos)
WERGO WER 6228–2

Sonata
Serenade in A
Peter Serkin (piano); with works by Peter Lieberson
and Stefan Wolpe
NEW WORLD NW 344–2

Vocal

Pastorale
Two Poems of Verlaine
Two Poems of Balmont
Three Japanese Lyrics
*Three Little Songs ('Recollections of my
    Childhood')*
Babel
Stuttgart Radio Symphony Orchestra and Choir
conducted by Gary Bertini; with Stravinsky's
Symphony of Psalms, Two Poems of Verlaine,
Abraham and Isaac and Elegy for J. F. K.
ORFEO C 015 821 A

Pribaoutki
Cat's Cradle Songs
Four Songs
Three Songs from William Shakespeare
'In memoriam Dylan Thomas'
Elegy for J.F.K.
Two Sacred Songs (after Wolf)
Phyllis Bryn-Julson (soprano), Ann Murray (mezzo-
soprano), Robert Tear (tenor), John Shirley-Quirk
(baritone); Ensemble InterContemporain conducted
by Pierre Boulez; with extract from Stravinsky's *Mavra*
DG 431 751–2GC

Symphony of Psalms
Czech Philharmonic Chorus and Orchestra conducted
by Karel Ančerl; with Stravinsky's *Oedipus Rex*
SUPRAPHON 11 1947–2

Mass
English Bach Festival Choir and Orchestra conducted
by Leonard Bernstein; with Stravinsky's *Les Noces*
DG 423 251–2GC

Canticum sacrum
John Mark Ainsley (tenor), Stephen Roberts
(baritone); Westminster Cathedral Choir and City of
London Sinfonia conducted by James O'Donnell; with
Stravinsky's Symphony of Psalms, Pater noster, Credo,
Ave Maria and Mass
HYPERION CDA 66437

Abraham and Isaac
Dietrich Fischer-Dieskau (baritone); Stuttgart Radio
Symphony Orchestra conducted by Gary Bertini;
with Stravinsky's Symphony of Psalms, Two Poems
of Verlaine, *Babel* and Elegy for J. F. K.
ORFEO C 015 821 A

Orchestral

The Song of the Nightingale
French National Orchestra conducted by Pierre
Boulez; with Stravinsky's *Pulcinella*
ERATO 2292–45382–2

Symphonies of Wind Instruments
Nash Ensemble conducted by Sir Simon Rattle; with
Stravinsky's Three Pieces for String Quartet, Two
Poems of Balmont, Three Japanese Lyrics, *Ragtime* and
other songs and piano pieces
Chandos CHAN 6535

Piano Concerto
Capriccio for Piano and Orchestra
'Movements' for Piano and Orchestra
Symphonies of Wind Instruments
Paul Crossley (piano); London Sinfonietta conducted
by Esa-Pekka Salonen
SONY SK 45797

Violin Concerto
David Oistrakh (violin); Lamoureux Orchestra
conducted by Bernard Haitink; with concerto
by Mozart
PHILIPS 434 167–2PM

Divertimento
Suites Nos. 1 and 2
London Sinfonietta conducted by Riccardo
Chailly; with Stravinsky's Octet and suite from
The Soldier's Tale
DECCA 433 079–2DM

Symphony in C
Symphony in Three Movements
Orchestre de la Suisse Romande conducted by Charles
Dutoit; with Stravinsky's *Scherzo fantastique* and
Symphonies of Wind Instruments
DECCA 436 474–2DM

Octet
Suite from 'The Soldier's Tale'
London Sinfonietta conducted by Riccardo Chailly;
with Stravinsky's *Divertimento*; Suites Nos. 1 and 2
DECCA 433 079–2DM

Chamber/Instrumental

Three Pieces for String Quartet
Concertino for String Quartet
Double Canon 'Raoul Dufy in memoriam'
Alban Berg String Quartet; with music by von Einem
EMI CDC7 54347–2

Index

Page numbers in italics refer to
picture captions.

**Photographic
Acknowledgements**

Archiv für Kunst und Geschichte,
    London: 30–1, 46, 137, 142
Ashmolean Museum, Oxford:
    66–7, 68
Bibliothèque nationale de France,
    Paris: 36, 49, 51, 62, 63, 97,
    102–3, 105, 125
Property of Robert Craft: 214
Photographie Giraudon, Paris:
    116–7
© David Hockney, 1975: 166–7
Hulton-Deutsch Collection,
    London: 11, 16, 20–1, 44, 91,
    126, 146, 154, 155, 159, 171, 173,
    177, 185, 191, 195, 196, 206–7,
    208–9, 211, 218–9
Hulton-Deutsch/photo by
    Erich Auerbach: 176, 182–3
Courtesy Estate of George Platt
    Lynes: 163
Magnum Photos Ltd: 199
The Mansell Collection, London:
    23, 148
Musée nationale d'art moderne,
    Paris: 178
Michael Larionov, Renard: design
    for scenery, 1921.
    Watercolour, 52.1 x 64.1 cm.
    The Museum of Modern Art,
    New York. Gift of the Artist.
    Photograph © 1994
    The Museum of Modern Art:
    80–1
By courtesy of the
    National Portrait Gallery,
    London: 147
Novosti: 19, 22, 197
Paul Sacher Foundation,
    Igor Stravinsky Archive:
    13, 14, 15, 26, 28, 50, 61, 101,
    109, 132, 135, 202, 21
Range Pictures Ltd, London: 139,
    140t, 193, 196
Photo © R.M.N., Paris: 73
    (Musée d'Orsay), 89, 93
    (Musée Picasso)
Roger-Viollet, Paris: 64–5, 99, 110,
    120–1
Royal Opera House Archive,
    Covent Garden/photograph by
    Hans Wild: 153
Photograph by R. Sawyer,
    Washington DC: 134
SCR Photo Library, London: 35
Sony Classical Photo Archives: 174
Photographs by Martha Swope,
    Time Magazine/Katz Pictures:
    186, 187, 188–9
Photograph by Houston Rogers,
    Theatre Museum/V&A,
    London: 127, 130–1, 201
Photograph by Denis de Marney,
    Theatre Museum/V&A,
    London: 150–1
Photograph by J.W. Debenham,
    Theatre Museum/V&A: 128
Theatre Museum/V&A, London:
    V&A: 41, 43, 79, 82, 84, 86–7,
    95, 112, 123, 123